Ordnance Survey
THE COMPLETE
Road Atlas
IRELAND

CW00348042

i	DISTANCE CHART - CONVERSION TABLES
ii	ROUTE PLANNER
iii	MOTORING INFORMATION, REPUBLIC OF IRELAND
iv	MOTORING INFORMATION, NORTHERN IRELAND
v	TRAVEL INFORMATION
vi	LEGEND TO NATIONAL MAPS

1-70 NATIONAL MAPS

TOWN MAPS

71	DUBLIN	80	LIMERICK	86	DOWNPATRICK DUNDALK	92	PORTRUSH ROSSLARE HBR
73	BELFAST	81	WATERFORD	87	ENNISKILLEN KILLARNEY	93	SLIGO TRALEE
75	CORK	82	ARMAGH ATHLONE	88	LARNE LETTERKENNY	94	WESTPORT WEXFORD
77	LONDONDERRY	83	BALLYMENA BANGOR	89	LISBURN MULLINGAR		
78	GALWAY	84	CASHEL COLERAINE	90	NEWCASTLE NEWRY		
79	KILKENNY	85	CRAIGAVON-LURGAN CRAIGAVON-PORTADOWN	91	NEWTOWNARDS OMAGH.		

95	TOURIST OFFICES
97	GOLF INFORMATION
99	GAZETTEER

INDEX TO MAP PAGES - INSIDE FRONT COVER

Compiled and published by the Director at Ordnance Survey Ireland, Phoenix Park, Dublin 8, Ireland
and the Director at the Ordnance Survey of Northern Ireland, Colby House, Stranmillis Court, Belfast, BT9 5BJ.

Distance Chart

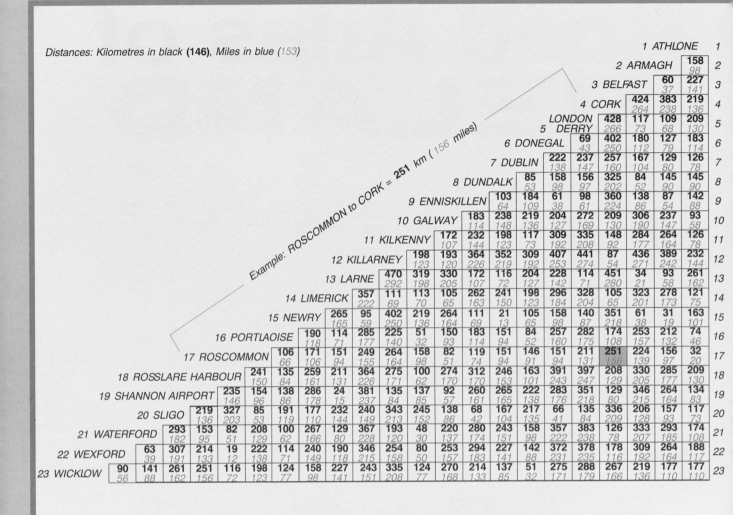

Distances: Kilometres in black (146), Miles in blue (153)

Example: ROSCOMMON to CORK = 251 km (156 miles)

(Triangular distance matrix between the following places: 1 ATHLONE, 2 ARMAGH, 3 BELFAST, 4 CORK, 5 LONDONDERRY/DERRY, 6 DONEGAL, 7 DUBLIN, 8 DUNDALK, 9 ENNISKILLEN, 10 GALWAY, 11 KILKENNY, 12 KILLARNEY, 13 LARNE, 14 LIMERICK, 15 NEWRY, 16 PORTLAOISE, 17 ROSCOMMON, 18 ROSSLARE HARBOUR, 19 SHANNON AIRPORT, 20 SLIGO, 21 WATERFORD, 22 WEXFORD, 23 WICKLOW.)

Conversion Tables

DISTANCES AND SPEED

1 Mile = 1.609344 Kms

1 Kilometre = 0.621371 Miles

1 Yard = 91.4 Cms

1 Foot = 30.5 Cms

1 Inch = 2.5 Cms

WEIGHTS

1 Pound = 0.45 Kilogrammes

1 Kilogramme = 2.20 Pounds

VOLUMES

0.5 Pint = 0.28 Litre

1 Pint = .57 Litre

1 Litre = 0.22 Gallon

PRESSURE

Pounds per sq. inch to kgs. per sq. cm.

ppi	kpc
26	1.83
28	1.96
30	2.10
32	2.24
36	2.52
40	2.80

TEMPERATURE

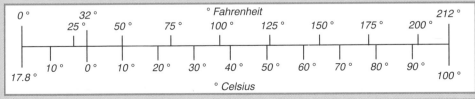

ROUTE PLANNER

ii

MOTORING INFORMATION
REPUBLIC OF IRELAND

DRIVING IS ON THE LEFT THROUGHOUT IRELAND.
SEAT BELTS must be worn by drivers and passengers.
CRASH HELMETS must be worn by motorcyclists and pillion passengers.

WARNING SIGNS

The following are examples of the principal signs.

TWO-WAY TRAFFIC

Dangerous Corner or Bend Ahead | Series of Dangerous Corners or Bends Ahead | Slippery Stretch of Road Ahead | Sharp Rise Ahead | Sharp Depression Ahead | Series of Bumps or Hollows Ahead

Junction Ahead With Road or Roads of Equal Importance. | Steep Ascent Ahead | Steep Descent Ahead | Road Narrows Dangerously | Roundabout Ahead

Junction Ahead With Roads of Less Importance. (minor roads shown by thin arms) | Unprotected Quay, Canal or River | Road Works Ahead | Children Sign (School etc.) | Traffic Lights Ahead

Junctions Ahead With Roads of Equal Importance | With Roads of Less Importance | Advanced Warning of a Major Road Ahead | Low Bridge Ahead | Level Crossing Ahead guarded by gates. | Level Crossing Ahead Unguarded. | End of Dual Carriageway.

REGULATORY SIGNS

These signs implement road regulations and show the course to follow etc.

Traffic must proceed in the direction of the arrow.

Keep to Left Carriageway

Traffic may not proceed in the direction of the arrow.

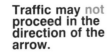

Give Way

YIELD RIGHT OF WAY

Parking
 Parking Permitted | Clearway Stopping or Parking Prohibited (except Buses and Taxis) | Parking Prohibited | TAXI RANK Parking for taxis only.

SPEED LIMITS

MOTORWAY
70 mph/112 kph.

NATIONAL LIMIT
60 mph/96 kph

OTHER LIMITS MAY APPLY IN TOWNS, BUILT-UP AREAS AND SOME ROADS AS INDICATED.

30 **40**
End of Speed Limit

INFORMATION SIGNS

These signs will give information regarding direction, distance, place etc.
Amenities of particular interest to tourists are displayed in white on a brown background.

Loch Garman N11 WEXFORD
Bré BRAY

N11 N7
N81
N4
N11

2 Bré BRAY
Cearnóg Mhuirfean Merrion Square 2
An Nás NAAS
4 km
2 km

NO L-drivers, Vehicles under 50 c.c., Slow vehicles (under 30 mph), Invalid-carriages, Pedal-cycles, Pedestrians, Animals.
Motorway ahead

M50 Entry to Motorway

Motorway ahead Motorway Regulations no longer apply

500m
Approaching end of Motorway

Eolas do Thurasóirí TOURIST INFORMATION
Slí na Bóinne BOYNE DRIVE

CONTROL ZONES
Cities and towns in Northern Ireland may have special parking and security restrictions in some areas - Control Zones - details of which are posted locally.

Control Zone — NO VEHICLE TO BE LEFT UNATTENDED — at any time

WARNING SIGNS

 Traffic merges from right

 Cross roads

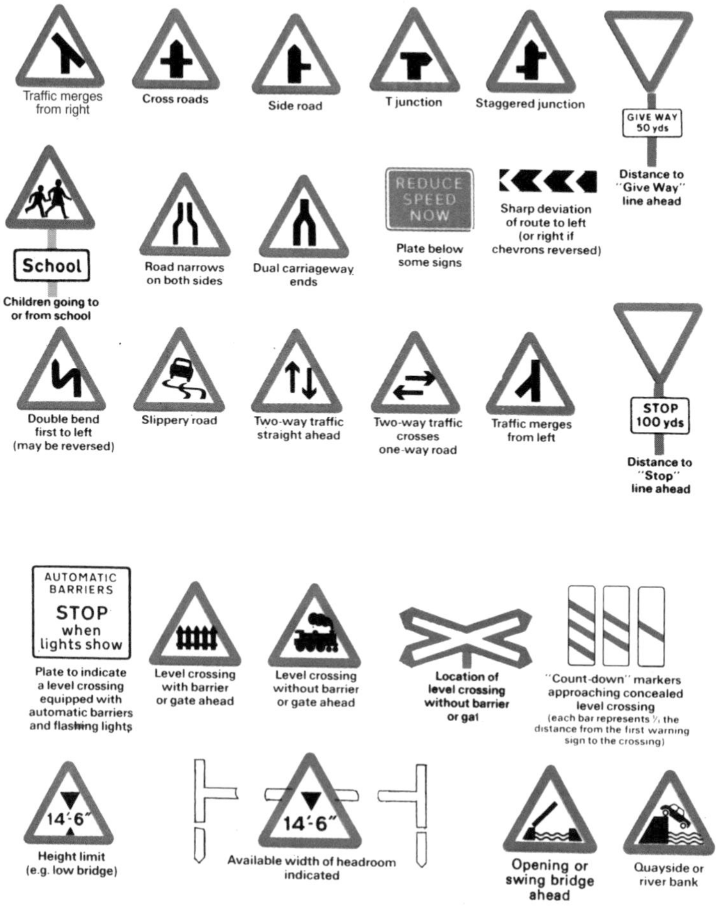

Side road

 T junction

 Staggered junction

 GIVE WAY 50 yds — Distance to "Give Way" line ahead

 School — Children going to or from school

 Road narrows on both sides

 Dual carriageway ends

 REDUCE SPEED NOW — Plate below some signs

 Sharp deviation of route to left (or right if chevrons reversed)

 STOP 100 yds — Distance to "Stop" line ahead

 Double bend first to left (may be reversed)

 Slippery road

 Two-way traffic straight ahead

 Two-way traffic crosses one-way road

 Traffic merges from left

 AUTOMATIC BARRIERS — STOP when lights show — Plate to indicate a level crossing equipped with automatic barriers and flashing lights

 Level crossing with barrier or gate ahead

Level crossing without barrier or gate ahead

 Location of level crossing without barrier or gate

 "Count-down" markers approaching concealed level crossing (each bar represents ⅓ the distance from the first warning sign to the crossing)

14'6" Height limit (e.g. low bridge)

14'6" Available width of headroom indicated

Opening or swing bridge ahead

Quayside or river bank

SIGNS GIVING ORDERS

These signs are mostly circular and those with red circles are mostly prohibitive

 40 — Maximum speed

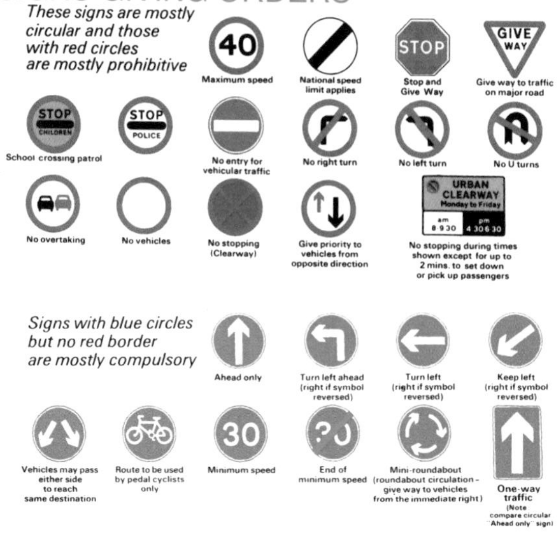

National speed limit applies

STOP — Stop and Give Way

GIVE WAY — Give way to traffic on major road

 STOP CHILDREN — School crossing patrol

 STOP POLICE

 No entry for vehicular traffic

 No right turn

No left turn

No U turns

 No overtaking

 No vehicles

No stopping (Clearway)

Give priority to vehicles from opposite direction

URBAN CLEARWAY Monday to Friday am 8 9.30 pm 4 30 6.30 — No stopping during times shown except for up to 2 mins. to set down or pick up passengers

Signs with blue circles but no red border are mostly compulsory

Ahead only

Turn left ahead (right if symbol reversed)

Turn left (right if symbol reversed)

Keep left (right if symbol reversed)

Vehicles may pass either side to reach same destination

Route to be used by pedal cyclists only

30 — Minimum speed

End of minimum speed

Mini-roundabout (roundabout circulation - give way to vehicles from the immediate right)

One-way traffic (Note compare circular 'Ahead only' sign)

DIRECTION SIGNS

Signs on motorways *Blue backgrounds*

 M1 — Start of motorway

 Belfast M2 / Ballyclare Larne Templepatrick A 57 — On approaches to junctions (junction number on black background)

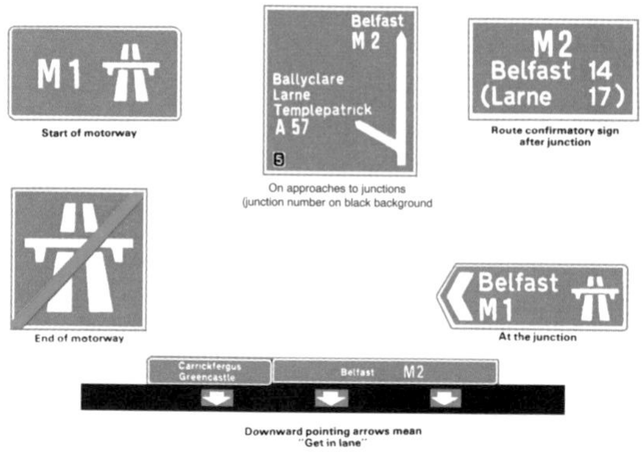

M2 Belfast 14 (Larne 17) — Route confirmatory sign after junction

 End of motorway

Belfast M1 — At the junction

Carrickfergus Greencastle / Belfast M2 — Downward pointing arrows mean "Get in lane"

DIRECTION SIGNS

Signs on primary routes *Green backgrounds*

 A 1 Belfast 24 Dromore 7 Lisburn 16 — Route confirmatory sign after junction

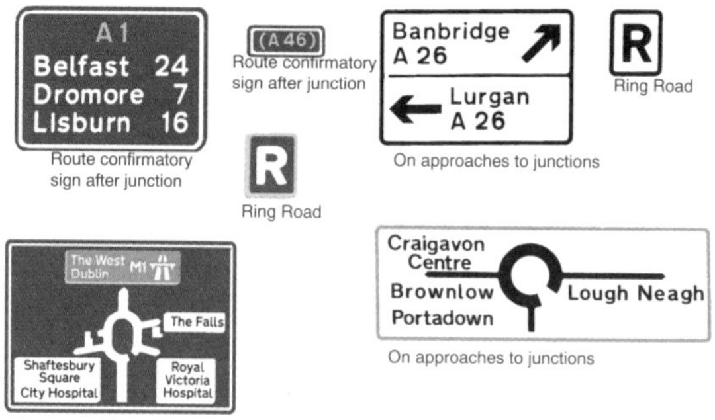

(A 46) — Route confirmatory sign after junction

 Banbridge A 26 / Lurgan A 26 — On approaches to junctions

Signs on non-primary routes *Black borders*

R — Ring Road

R — Ring Road

Craigavon Centre / Brownlow / Portadown — Lough Neagh — On approaches to junctions

 The West Dublin M1 / The Falls / Shaftesbury Square City Hospital / Royal Victoria Hospital — On approaches to junctions (The blue panel indicates that the motorway commences from the junction ahead. The motorway shown in brackets can also be reached by proceeding in that direction.)

INFORMATION SIGNS

 ONE WAY — One-way street

 Priority over vehicles from opposite direction

 No through road

 H Hospital — Hospital ahead

 P — Parking place; plate may indicate any restrictions on use

 Forton Services — Direction to service area with fuel, parking, cafeteria and restaurant facilities

 "Count-down" markers at exit from motorway (each bar represents 100 yards to the exit) Green-backed markers may be used on primary routes

 Appropriate traffic lanes at junction ahead

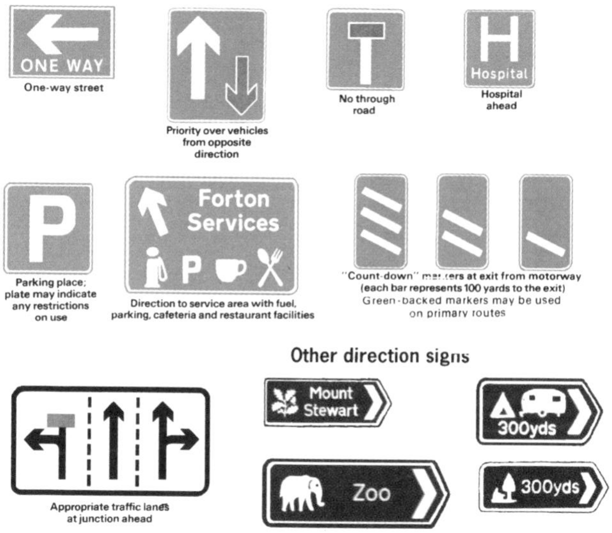

Other direction signs

 Mount Stewart

 Zoo

 300yds

300yds

WEATHER INFORMATION

| METCALL | 0336 444 900 |
| MARINECALL | 0870 600 4242 |

ROAD INFORMATION

MOTORING ORGANIZATIONS GENERAL ENQUIRIES
AA 0990 500 600
RAC 0870 572 2722

TRAVEL INFORMATION REPUBLIC OF IRELAND

BUS

Bus Atha Cliath - Dublin Bus	(01)	8734222
Bus Eireann - Irish Bus	(01)	8366111
ATHLONE	(0902)	73322
BALLINA	(096)	71800
BALLYSHANNON	(072)	51101
CAVAN	(049)	4331353
CORK	(021)	4508188
DROGHEDA	(041)	9835023
DUBLIN	(01)	8366111
DUNDALK	(042)	9334075
ENNIS	(065)	6824177
GALWAY	(091)	562000
KILLARNEY	(064)	30011
LETTERKENNY	(074)	21309
LIMERICK	(061)	313333
LONGFORD	(043)	45208
MONAGHAN	(047)	82377
ROSSLARE HARBOUR	(053)	33114
SLIGO	(071)	60066
STRANORLAR	(074)	31008
TRALEE	(066)	7123566
WATERFORD	(051)	8790000

RAIL

IARNROD EIREANN	(01)	8366222
IRISH RAIL (including DART surburban rail).		

AIR

Arrivals and departures enquiries (same day only)

DUBLIN AIRPORT	(01)	8141111
CORK AIRPORT		
(0715- 2300 hours)	(021)	4313131
(2300- 0700 hours)	(021)	4313288
SHANNON AIRPORT	(061)	471444
CONNAUGHT INT. AIRPORT	(094)	67222
DONEGAL AIRPORT	(075)	48232
KERRY AIRPORT	(066)	9764644
SLIGO AIRPORT	(071)	68280
WATERFORD AIRPORT	(051)	875589

SEA

STENA LINE		
Reservations LoCall	1890	313131
DUBLIN	(01)	2047777
DUN LAOGHAIRE	(01)	2047700
ROSSLARE	(053)	33115
CORK	(021)	272965
LIMERICK	(061)	316259
IRISH FERRIES		
DUBLIN	(01)	8552222
ROSSLARE	(053)	33158
CORK	(021)	4551995
BRITTANY FERRIES, CORK	(021)	4277801
SWANSEA / CORK FERRIES	(021)	4271166
ISLE OF MAN STEAM PACKET COMPANY		
	(01)	8364019
LoCall	1800	551743

TRAVEL INFORMATION NORTHERN IRELAND

AIR

BELFAST INTERNATIONAL	(028)	94422888
BELFAST CITY	(028)	90457745
CITY OF DERRY	(028)	71810784
ENNISKILLEN AIRPORT	(028)	66322771

RAIL

NORTHERN IRELAND RAILWAYS		
	(028)	90899411

SEA

STENA LINE	(08705)	707070
P&O IRISH-SEA	(0870)	2424777
SEACAT	(08705)	523523
NORSE IRISH FERRIES	(028)	90779090
ISLE OF MAN STEAM PACKET COMPANY		
	(08705)	523523
BELFAST FREIGHT FERRIES	(028)	90770112

BUS

ULSTERBUS HOTLINE	(028)	90333000

OUTSIDE HOTLINE HOURS

MON. - FRI.	0730 - 2030 hours
SATURDAY	0900 - 1800 hours
SUNDAY	0900 - 1930 hours

EUROPA BUS CENTRE	(028)	90320574
LAGANSIDE BUS CENTRE	(028)	90232356
CITYBUS	(028)	90246485

SCÁLA 1:210 000   SCALE 1:210 000

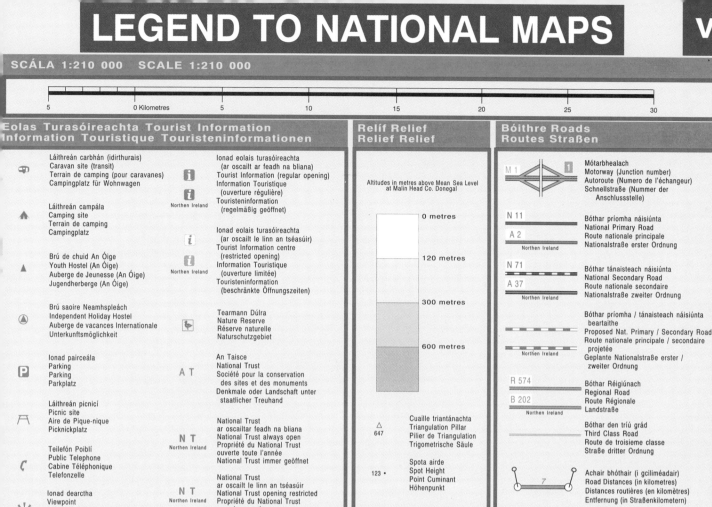

Eolas Turasóireachta Tourist Information
Information Touristique Touristeninformationen

Láithreán carbhán (idirthurais)
Caravan site (transit)
Terrain de camping (pour caravanes)
Campingplatz für Wohnwagen

Láithreán campála
Camping site
Terrain de camping
Campingplatz

Brú de chuid An Óige
Youth Hostel (An Óige)
Auberge de Jeunesse (An Óige)
Jugendherberge (An Óige)

Brú saoire Neamhspleách
Independent Holiday Hostel
Auberge de vacances Internationale
Unterkunftsmöglichkeit

Ionad páirceála
Parking
Parking
Parkplatz

Láithreán picnicí
Picnic site
Aire de Pique-nique
Picknickplatz

Teileafón Poiblí
Public Telephone
Cabine Téléphonique
Telefonzelle

Ionad dearctha
Viewpoint
Point de vue
Aussichtspunkt

Ionad eolais turasóireachta
(ar oscailt ar feadh na bliana)
Tourist Information (regular opening)
Information Touristique
(ouverture régulière)
Touristeninformation
(regelmäßig geöffnet)
Northen Ireland

Ionad eolais turasóireachta
(ar oscailt le linn an tséasúir)
Tourist Information centre
(restricted opening)
Information Touristique
(ouverture limitée)
Touristeninformation
(beschränkte Öffnungszeiten)
Northen Ireland

Tearmann Dúlra
Nature Reserve
Réserve naturelle
Naturschutzgebiet

An Taisce
National Trust
Société pour la conservation
des sites et des monuments
Denkmale oder Landschaft unter
staatlicher Treuhand

A T

National Trust
ar oscailtar feadh na bliana
National Trust always open
Propriété du National Trust
ouverte toute l'année
National Trust immer geöffnet
N T Northern Ireland

National Trust
ar oscailt le linn an tséasúir
National Trust opening restricted
Propriété du National Trust
ouverte en saison
National Trust nur während
der saison geöffnet
N T Northen Ireland

Relíf Relief
Relief Relief

Altitudes in metres above Mean Sea Level
at Malin Head Co. Donegal

0 metres
120 metres
300 metres
600 metres

△ 647   Cuaille triantánachta
Triangulation Pillar
Pilier de Triangulation
Trigometrische Säule

123 •   Spota airde
Spot Height
Point Cuminant
Höhenpunkt

Bóithre Roads
Routes Straßen

M 1   ▮ 1   Mótarbhealach
Motorway (Junction number)
Autoroute (Numero de l'échangeur)
Schnellstraße (Nummer der
Anschlussstelle)

N 11
A 2 Northen Ireland
Bóthar príomha náisiúnta
National Primary Road
Route nationale principale
Nationalstraße erster Ordnung

N 71
A 37 Northen Ireland
Bóthar tánaisteach náisiúnta
National Secondary Road
Route nationale secondaire
Nationalstraße zweiter Ordnung

Bóthar príomha / tánaisteach náisiúnta
beartaithe
Proposed Nat. Primary / Secondary Road
Route nationale principale / secondaire
projetée
Geplante Nationalstraße erster /
zweiter Ordnung
Northen Ireland

R 574
B 202 Northen Ireland
Bóthar Réigiúnach
Regional Road
Route Régionale
Landstraße

Bóthar den tríú grád
Third Class Road
Route de troisieme classe
Straße dritter Ordnung

7   Achair bhóthair (i gciliméadair)
Road Distances (in kilometres)
Distances routières (en kilomètres)
Entfernung (in Straßenkilometern)

In Northern Ireland roads are designated by the letter
A, B or M .
In the Republic of Ireland roads are designated by the
letter N, R or M.
The representation on these maps of a Road, Track or Path is
no evidence of a right of way.

Gnéithe ginearálta General features Traits généreaux Signaturen

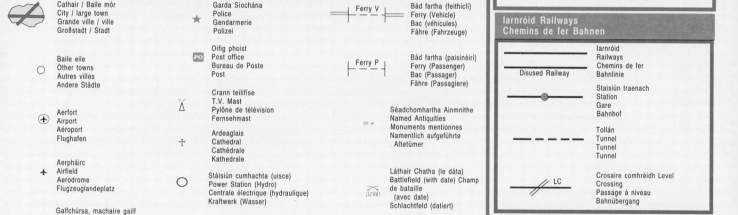

Cathair / Baile mór
City / large town
Grande ville / ville
Großstadt / Stadt

Baile eile
Other towns
Autres villes
Andere Städte

Aerfort
Airport
Aéroport
Flughafen

Aerpháirc
Airfield
Aerodrome
Flugzeuglandeplatz

Galfchúrsa, machaire gailf
Golf Course or Links
Terrain de Golf
Golfplatz oder Golfbahnen
9   18

Garda Síochána
Police
Gendarmerie
Polizei
★

Oifig phoist
Post office
Bureau de Poste
Post
PO

Crann teilifíse
T.V. Mast
Pylône de télévision
Fernsehmast

Ardeaglais
Cathedral
Cathédrale
Kathedrale
✝

Stáisiún cumhachta (uisce)
Power Station (Hydro)
Centrale électrique (hydraulique)
Kraftwerk (Wasser)
○

Stáisiún cumhachta (breosla iontaiseach)
Power Station (Fossil)
Centrale électrique (fossile)
Kraftwerk (fossile Brennstoffe)
◉

Ferry V
Bád fartha (feithiclí)
Ferry (Vehicle)
Bac (véhicules)
Fähre (Fahrzeuge)

Ferry P
Bád fartha (paisinéirí)
Ferry (Passenger)
Bac (Passager)
Fähre (Passagiere)

CH ⊕   Séadchomhartha Ainmnithe
Named Antiquities
Monuments mentionnes
Namentlich aufgeführte
Altetümer

Láthair Chatha (le dáta)
Battlefield (with date) Champ
de bataille
(avec date)
Schlachtfeld (datiert)
(1798)

Iarnróid Railways
Chemins de fer Bahnen

Disused Railway
Iarnróid
Railways
Chemins de fer
Bahnlinie

Staisiún traenach
Station
Gare
Bahnhof

Tollán
Tunnel
Tunnel
Tunnel

LC   Crosaire comhréidh Level
Crossing
Passage á niveau
Bahnübergang

Gnéithe uiscí Water features
Traits aquatiques Gewasserzeichen

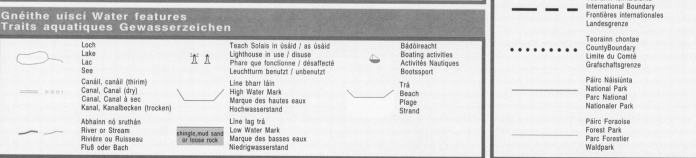

Loch
Lake
Lac
See

Canáil, canáil (thirim)
Canal, Canal (dry)
Canal, Canal à sec
Kanal, Kanalbecken (trocken)

Abhainn nó sruthán
River or Stream
Riviére ou Ruisseau
Fluß oder Bach

Teach Solais in úsáid / as úsáid
Lighthouse in use / disuse
Phare que fonctionne / désaffecté
Leuchtturm benutzt / unbenutzt

Line bharr láin
High Water Mark
Marque des hautes eaux
Hochwasserstand

Líne lag trá
Low Water Mark
Marque des basses eaux
Niedrigwasserstand

shingle,mud sand
or loose rock

Bádóireacht
Boating activities
Activités Nautiques
Bootssport

Trá
Beach
Plage
Strand

Teorainneacha Boundaries Frontières Grenzen

Teorainn idirnáisiúnta
International Boundary
Frontières internationales
Landesgrenze

Teorainn chontae
CountyBoundary
Limite du Comté
Grafschaftsgrenze

Páirc Náisiúnta
National Park
Parc National
Nationaler Park

Páirc Foraoise
Forest Park
Parc Forestier
Waldpark

TORY ISLAND
TORAIGH

West Town
Baile Thiar

East Town
Baile Thoir

TORY SOUND

Inishbeg

Inishdooey

Inishbofin
Inis Bó Finne

Ferry (P)

Ferry (P)

BLOODY FORELAND
CNOC FOLA

R257

Meenaclady
Mín an Chladaigh

6

3
Meenlaragh
Mín Larach

6

Brinlack
Bun na Leaca

Inishsirrer

Inishmeane

7

GWEEDORE
Gaoth Dobhair

L Lagha

OCEAN

Gola Island
Gabla

Gweedore
Bay

Derrybeg
Doirí Beaga

Tievealehid

Taobh an Leithid

431

The Stag Rocks

Inishinny

9
2

Gweedore
Gaoth Dobhair

R258

Inishfree
Lower

ATLANTIC

Owey Island

Uaigh

Inishfree
Bay

Bunbeg
An Bun Beag

R257b

5

N56

P
3

L Nacung
Loch na Cuing

Cruit
Island
An Chruit

Rinnafarset

R266

4

R259

Crolly

Grogan More

9

Kincaslough
Cionn Caslach

8

Annagary
Anagaire

Crocknafarragh

Torneady Point

Rosses Bay

5

Loughanure

A T

Ferry

9

ARAN ISLAND
ARAINN MHÓR

BURTONPORT
Ailt an Chorráin

THE ROSSES
Na Rosa

Lough
Anure

Leabgarrow
An Leadhb Gharbh

Meenbannad

7

Owenator River

R260

L Meela

8

Rutland
Island

N56

Crocknasharr
Crocknahallin

Inishkeeragh

R259

L Craghy

Lough
Croangar

Inishfree Upper

DUNGLOW
An Clochán Liath

13

Termon

Maghery
An Machair

Crohy Head

Alack
More

R252

E   F   G   H   **6**

❶

❷

NORTH CHANNEL

❸

P Torr Head

rnanmore
△ 379

Runabay Head
Carnaneigh
Loughareema
B92

Cushendun
Bun Abhann Duinne
Glendun
Viaduct
Glencorp

A2
Ossian's
Grave
⑨ Cushendall
Bun Abhann Dalla
RED BAY

ballyemon
Glenariff or Waterfoot
Gleann Aireamh

B14
A2
Garron Point
Knockore
A43
Glenariff
17
P
❹

Glenariff
rest Park
Hunters Point

Dungonnell
Dam
Carnlough
Carnlach
P
Straidkilly Point
llin Top
3
GLENARM
Gleann Arma

Glencloy
Glenarm
11
barns Hill
12
Drumnagreagh Port
P
10
A42
B97
The Maidens or
Hulin Rocks
Black Hill
P
❺

P
Scawt Hill
11
The
Sheddings
E
albanagh
Sheddings
kna
F
A2
P Ballygalley
Baile Geithligh
18
12
G

CAIRNRYAN (V)   FLEETWOOD (V)

H

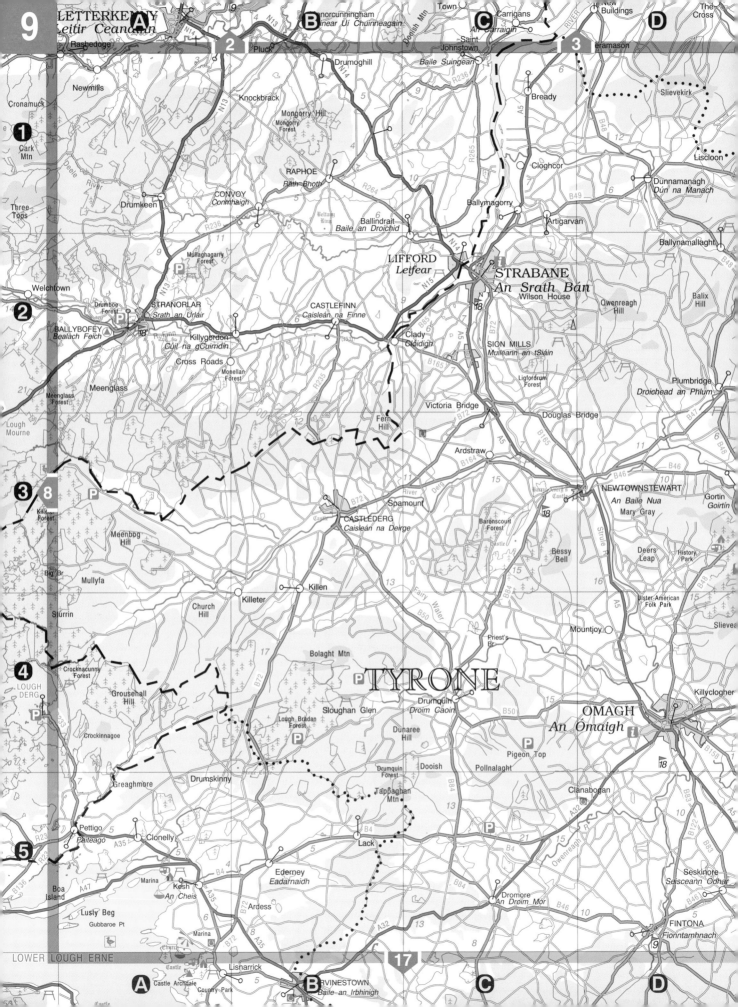

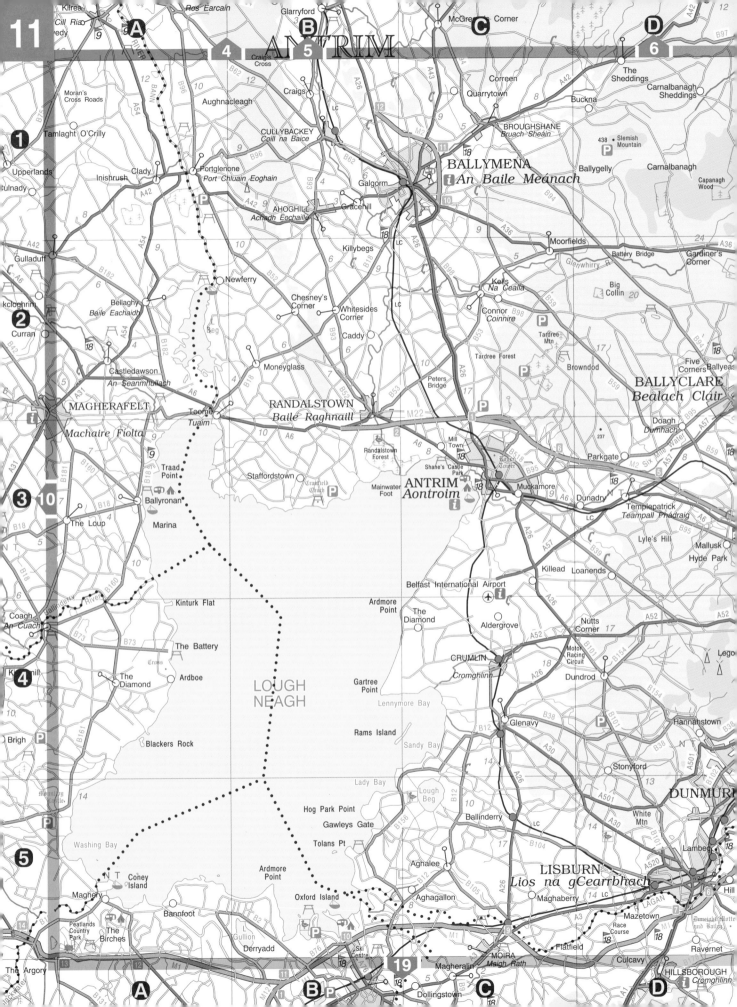

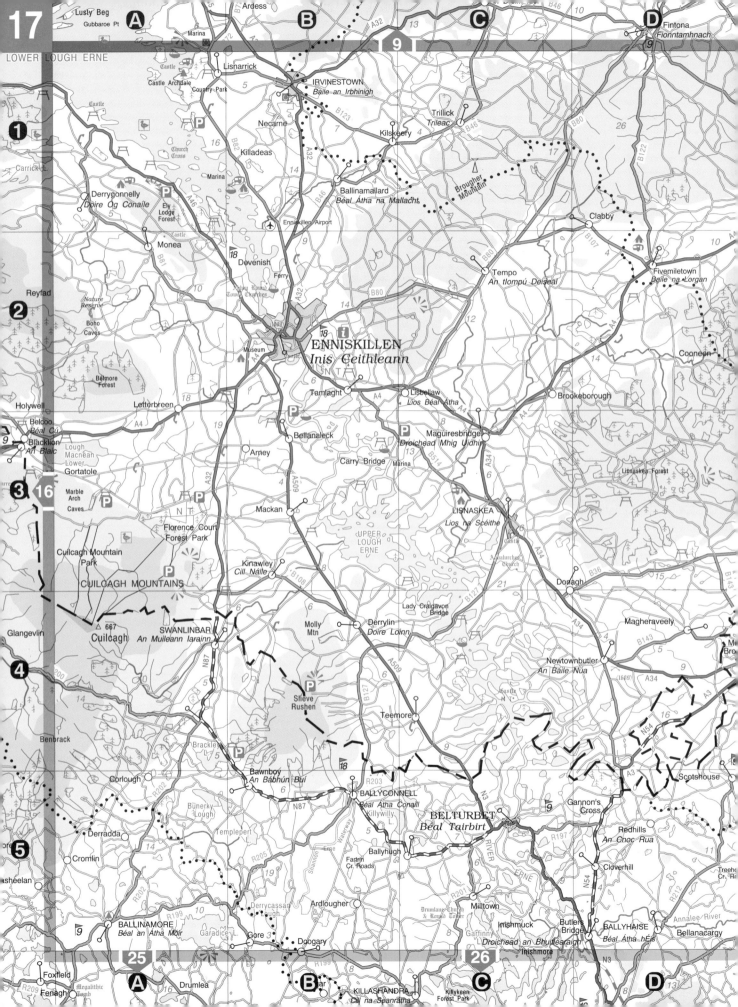

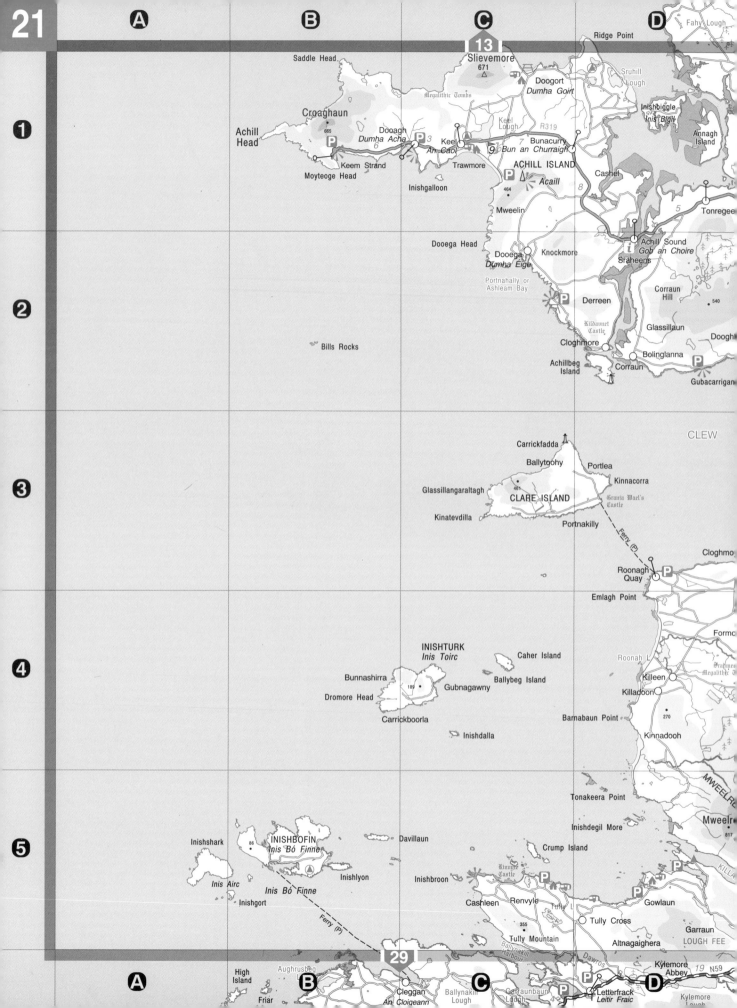

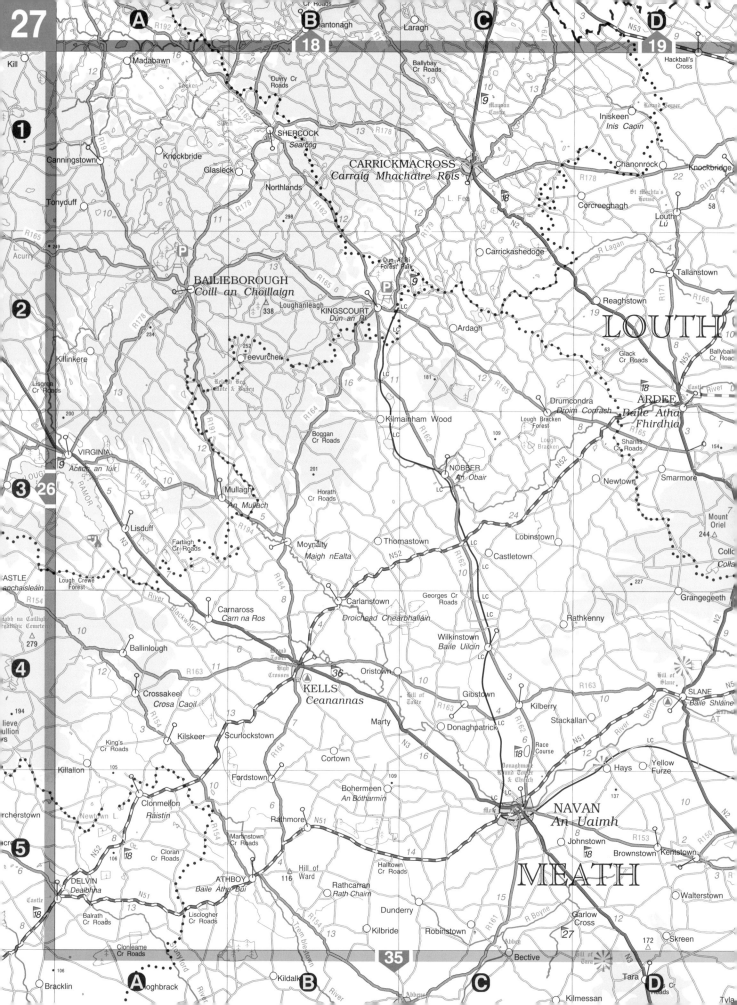

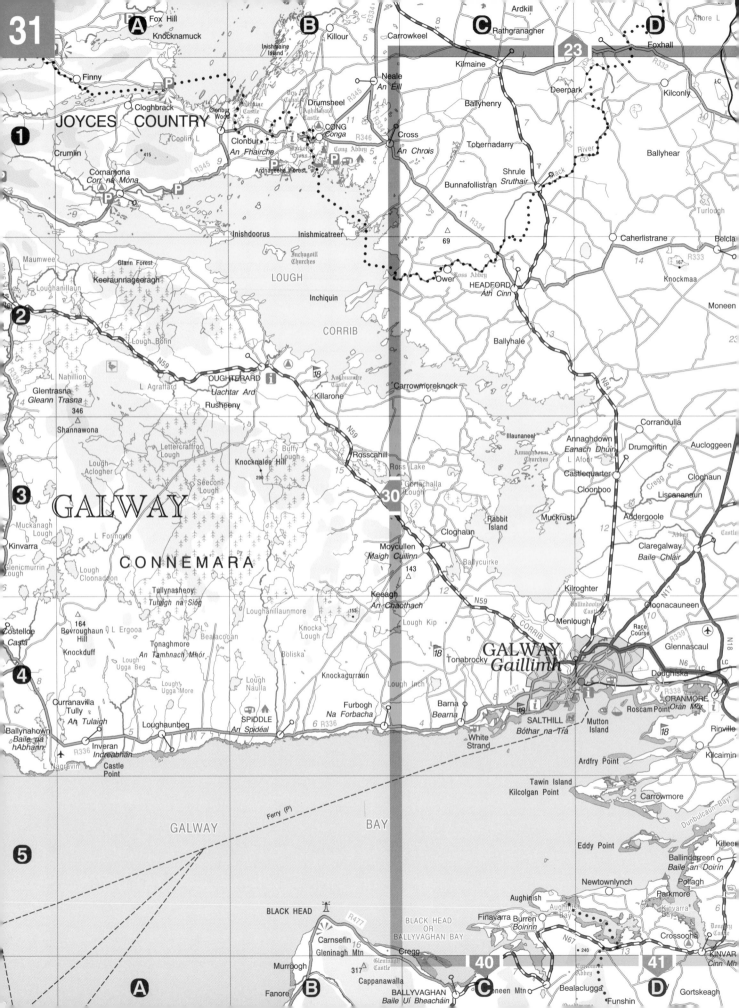

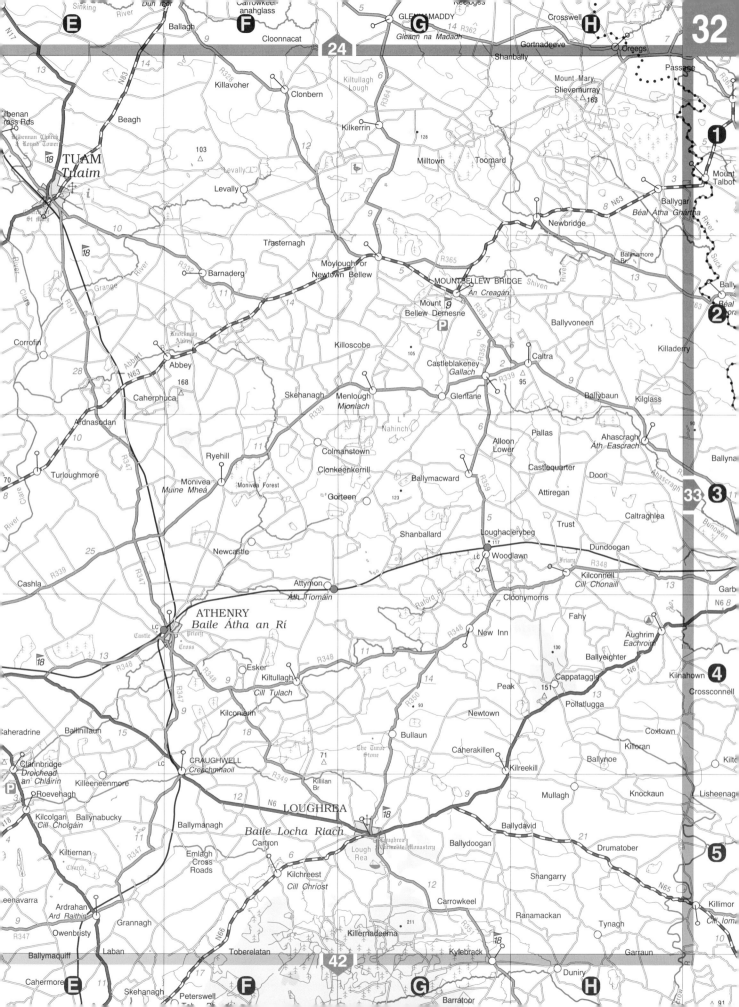

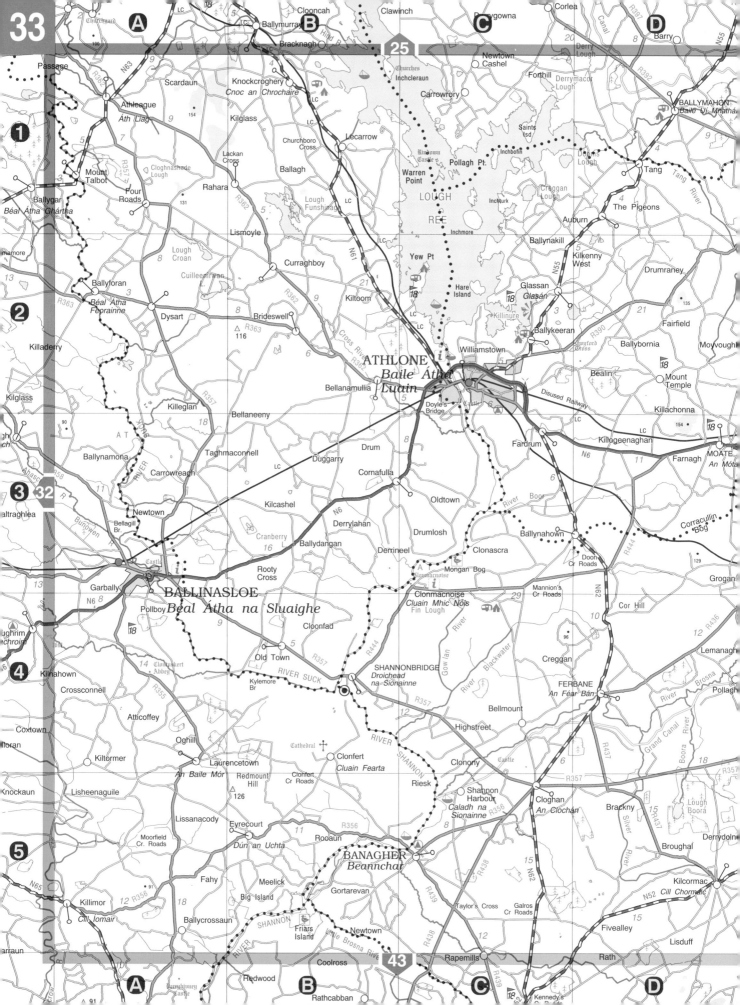

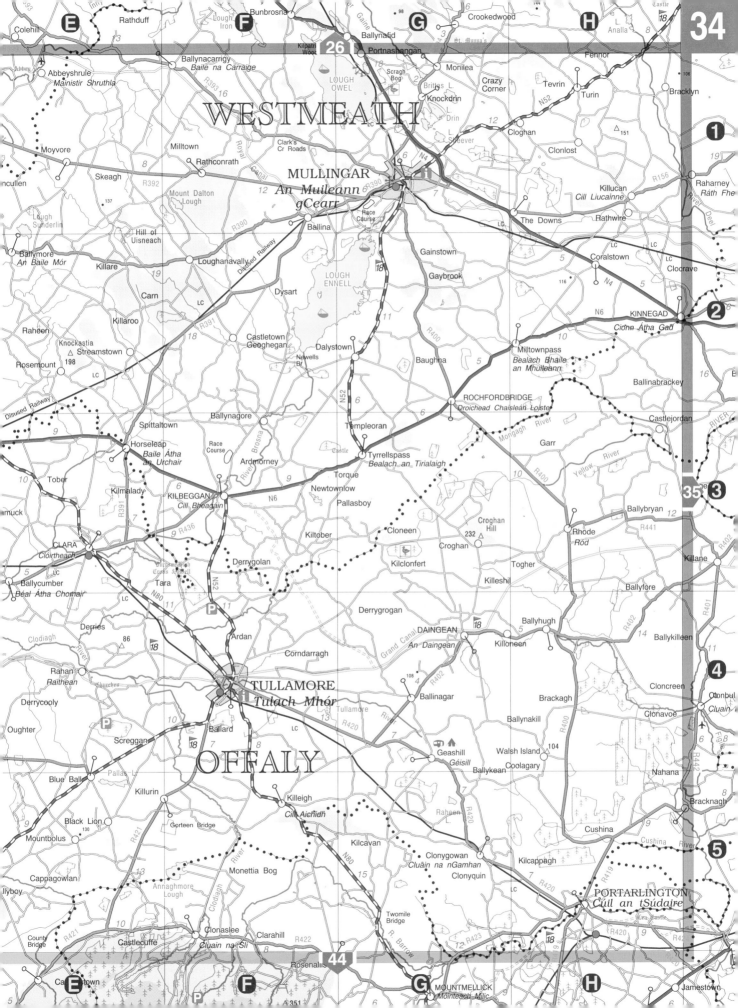

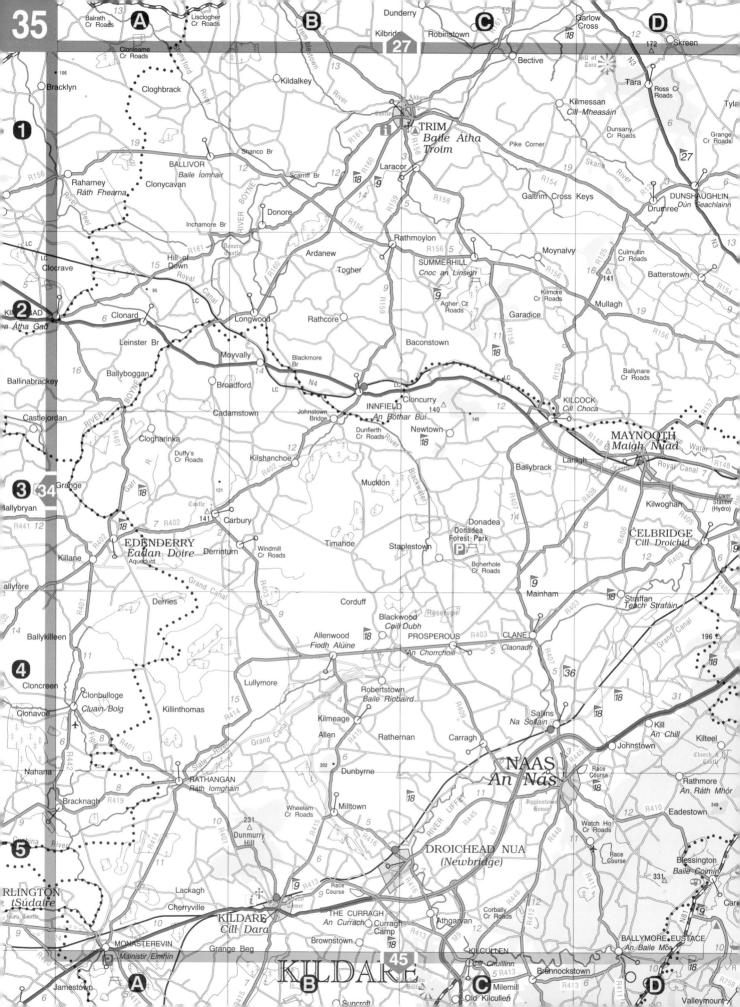

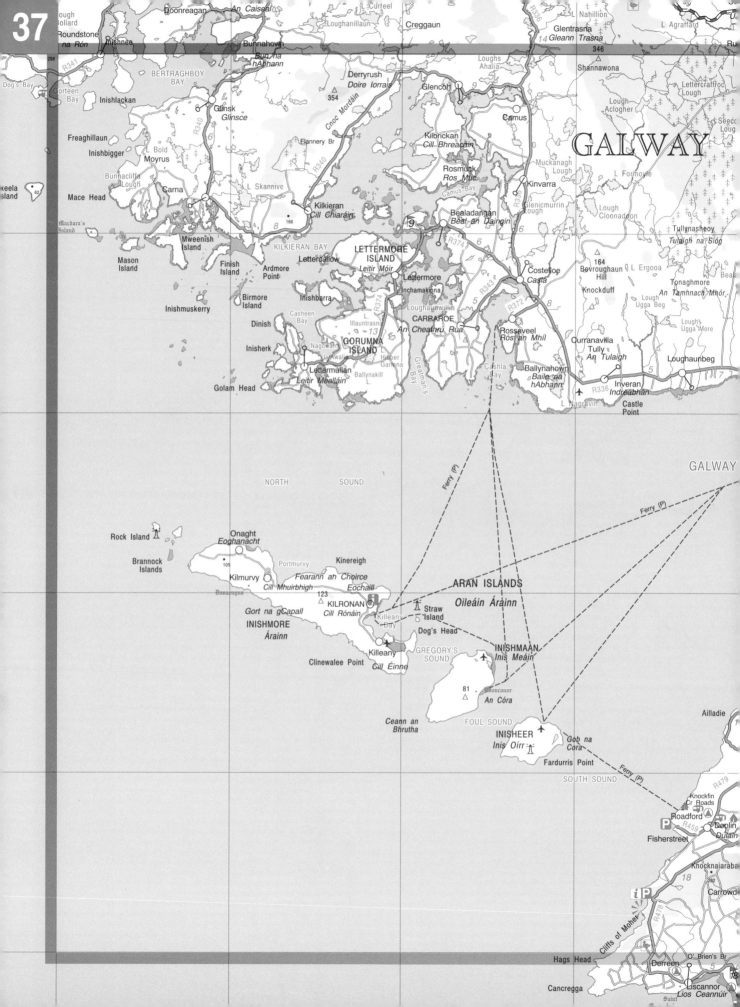

ATLANTIC OCEAN

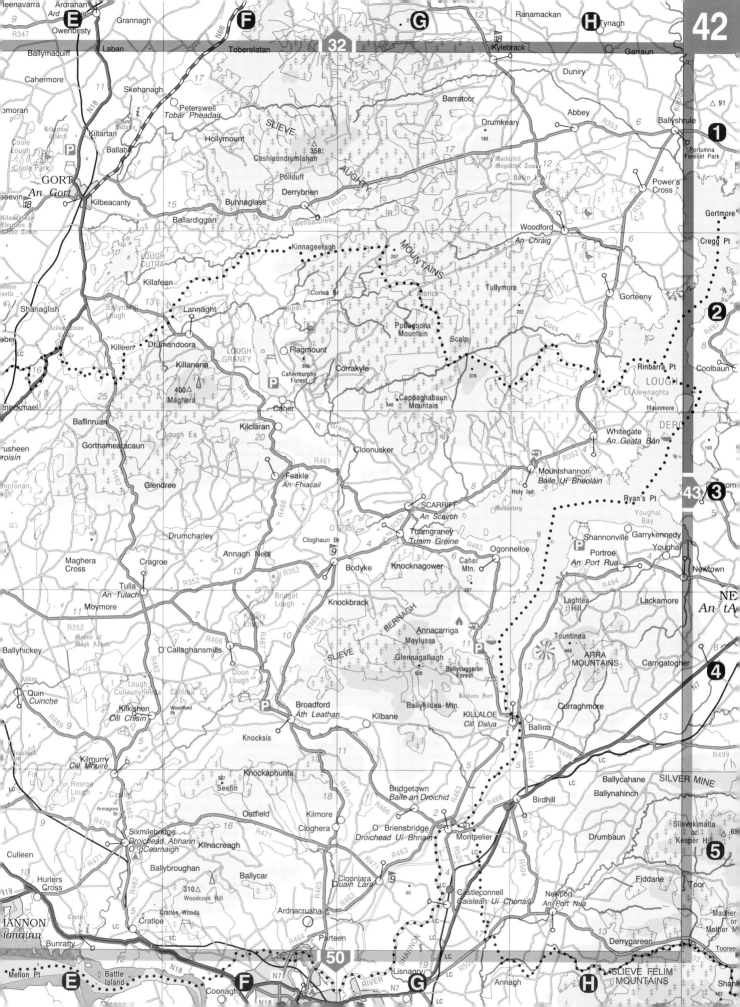

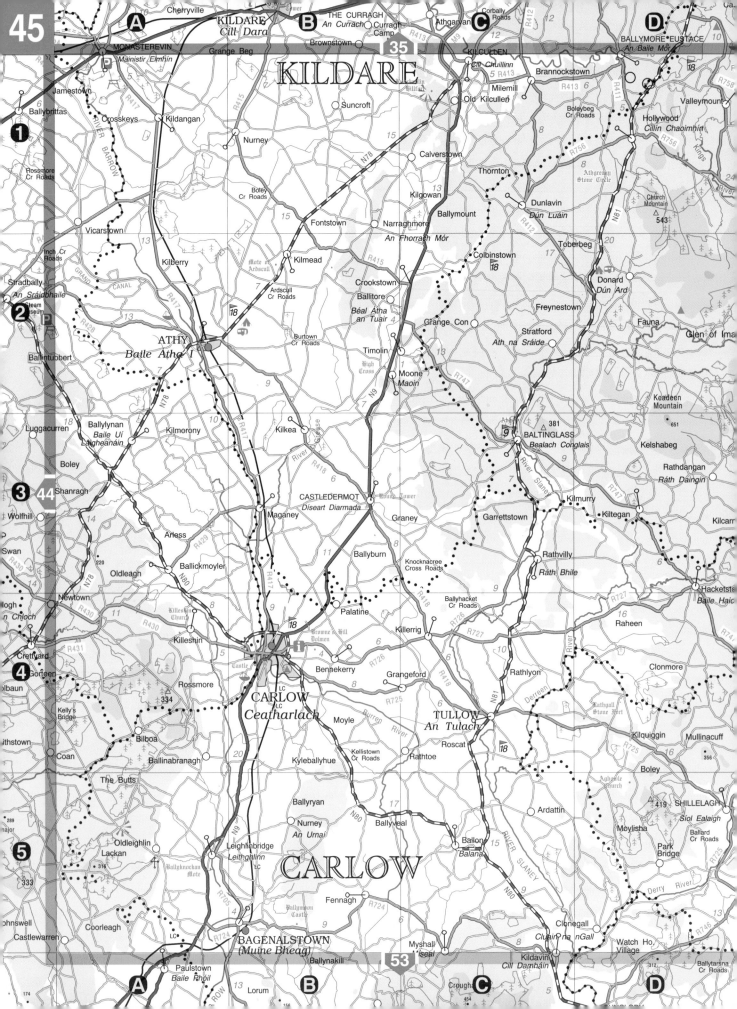

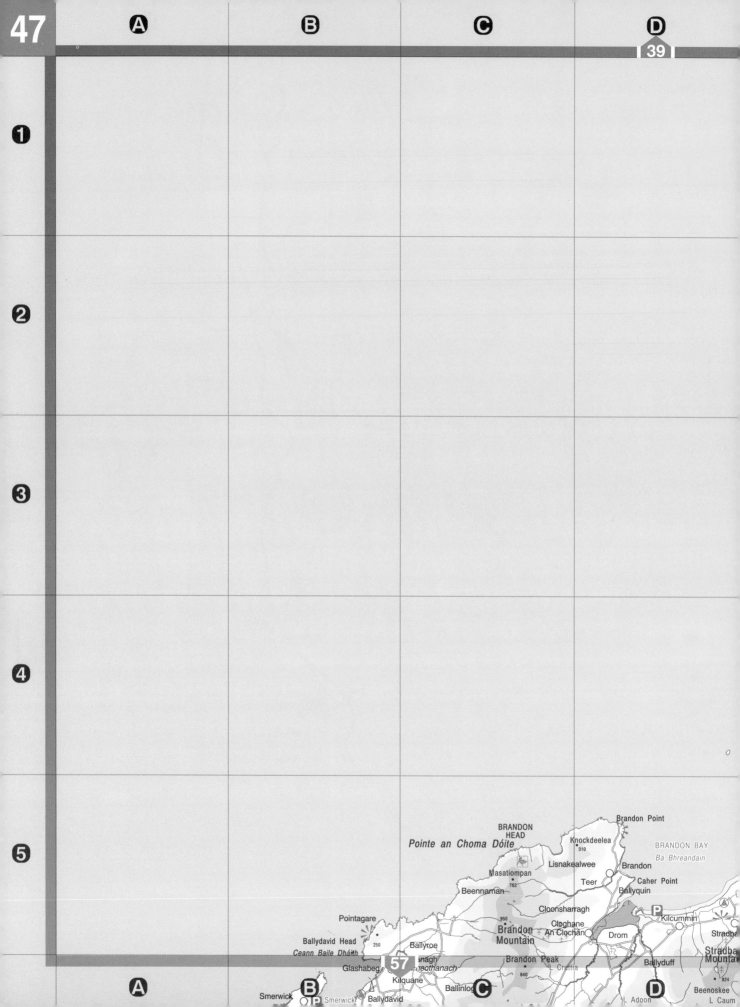

❶

❷

❸

❹

❺

BRANDON POINT

BRANDON HEAD
Pointe an Choma Dóite

Knockdeelea
310

BRANDON BAY
Bá Bhreandain

Lisnakealwee

Masatiompan
762

Brandon

Teer

Caher Point

Beennaman

Ballyquin

Cloonsharragh

Pointagare

Cloghane
An Clochán

Kilcummin

Ballydavid Head
Ceann Baile Dháith

250

Ballyroe

950
Brandon
Mountain

Drom

Stradba

P

Glashabeg

57

nagh
neothanach

Brandon Peak
840

L Cruttia

Ballyduff

Stradba
Mountan

A

Smerwick

B

P Smerwick

Ballydavid

Kilquane

Ballinlog

C

Ballynog

D

L Adoon

924
Beenoskee
L Caum

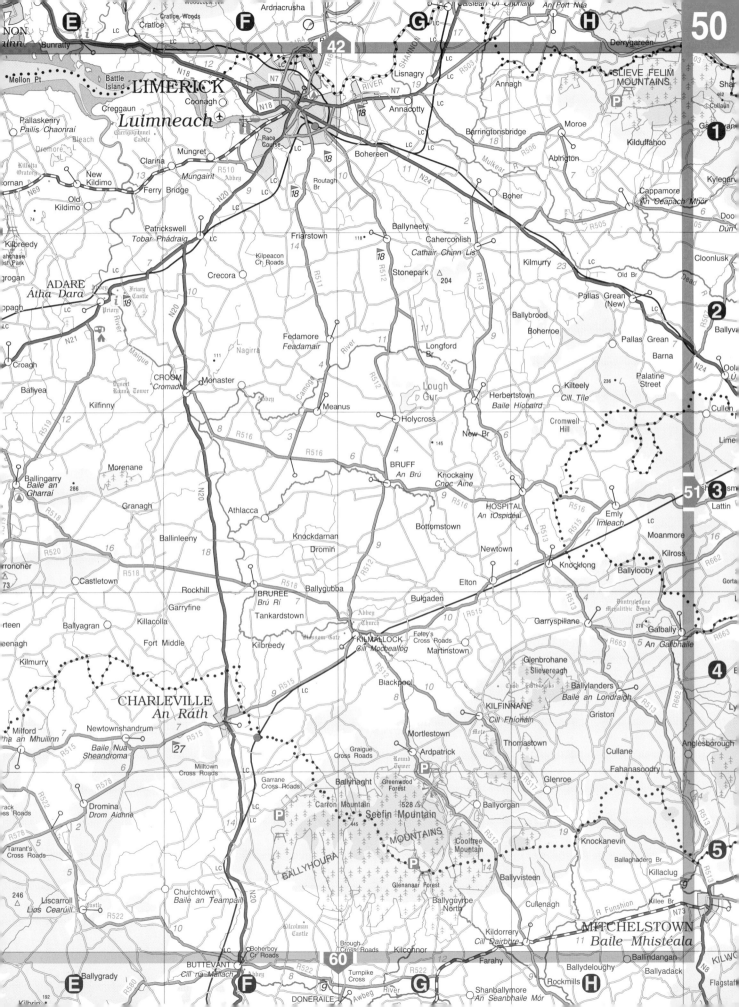

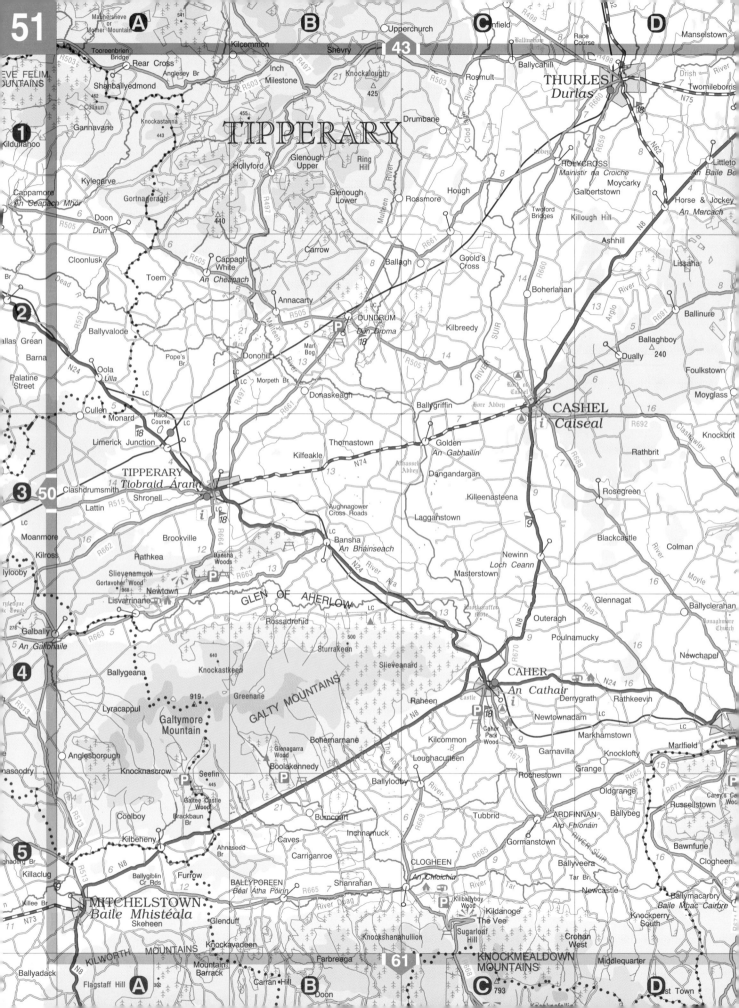

BRANDON HEAD
Pointe an Choma Dóite
Brandon Point
Knockdeelea
310
BRANDON BAY
Bá Bhreandain
Lisnakealwee
Brandon
Caher Point
Masatiompan
762
Teer
Ballyquin
Beennaman
Cloonsharragh
Cloghane
An Clochán
Drom
Kilcummin
Stradba
Stradba
Mount
Pointagare
Brandon
Mountain
950
Ballyroe
Feohanagh
An Fheothanach
Brandon Peak
840
Ballyduff
Glashabeg
Kilquane
L. Cruttia
Ballydavid Head
Ceann Baile Dháith
250
Smerwick
Smerwick Harbour
Ballydavid
Baile na nGall
Ballinloghig
DINGLE
L Gal
L Adoon
Beenoskee
824
L Caum
Sybil Head
17
Kilmalkedar
Ballysitteragh
Araglen
486
Slievenagower
Forest
Loug
Ansc
An Óir
Murreagh
An Mhúlríoch
622
Conair
615
Slievanea
Coumanare
Lakes
Sybil Point
18
Ballinrannig
Gallarus (Oratory)
Ballynana
Knockmoylemore
Coumduff
BALLYFERRITER
Baile an Fheirtearaigh
Knockavrogeen
Ballybowler
Lisdargan
Annagap
ANASCAUL
Clogher Head
Teeravane
Ballineanig
R559
403
Ballyeightragh
Milltown
Baile an Mhuilinn
8
Lispole
Lios Póil
Abhainn an Scáil
Croaghmarhin
Ventry
DINGLE
An Daingean
N86
9
Dunquin
Dún Chaoin
R559
7
Aglish
9
Kildurrihy
Dingle Harbour
Doonmanagh
284
Acres Point
Inishtooskert
172
Mount Eagle
514
Ventry Harbour
Ballymacadoyle Hill
Reenbeg Point
Bull's Head
Minard Head
Gubranna
Beginish
BLASKET SOUND
Beenacouma
Fahan
Parkmore Pt
GREAT BLASKET ISLAND
Garraun Pt
Cloghans
An Blascaod Mór
290
SLEA HEAD
Ceann Sléibhe
14
Dunbeg (Promontory Fort)
Tearaght Island
Canduff
DINGLE BAY
Bá an Daingin
175
Inishnabro
139
Inishvickillane
Ferry (P) Seasonal
King's Head
Gleensk Wood
Beenn
Darby's Br
Kells
Mount Foley
Killurly Commons
Been Hill
662
Mullaghnara
Canglass Point
688
Knocknadobar
N70
12
Coosfadda
Slievagh
Castlequin
Foilmore Br
Teeromoyl
Killelan Mountain
Leacanabuaile Stone Fort
Coomduff
495
Caunoge
DOULUS HEAD
CAHERSIVEEN
Cathair Saidhbhín
Knockaheden Cross
Beginish Island
Reenadrolaun Pt
Island
Reenard Cross
Keelnagore
VALENCIA HARBOUR
Fogher Cliff
Knights Town

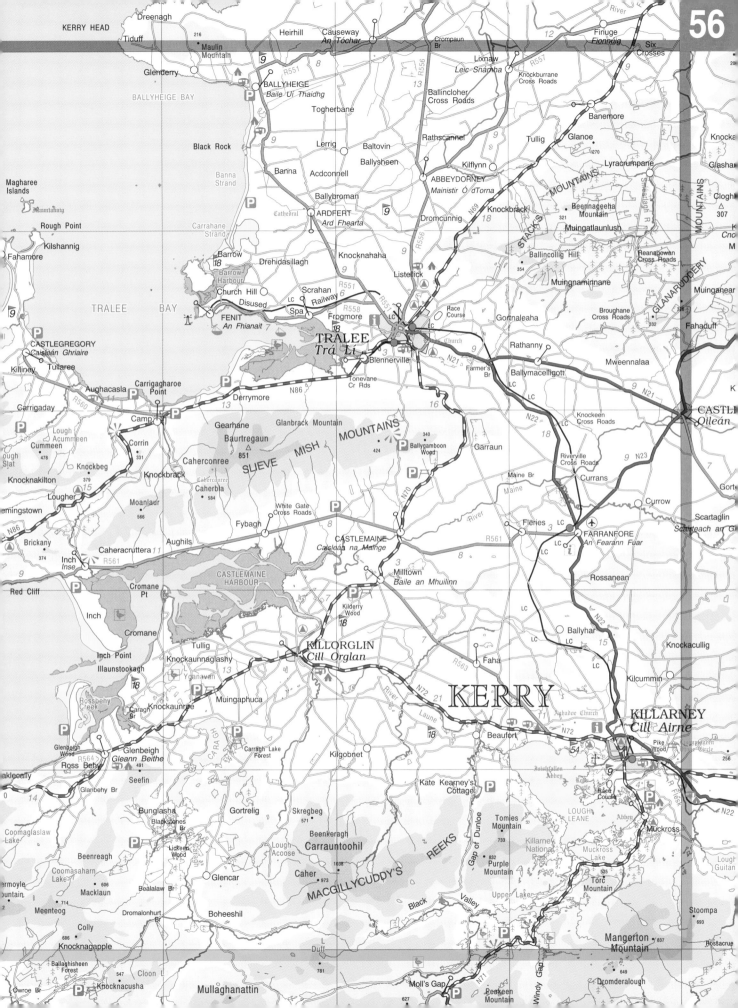

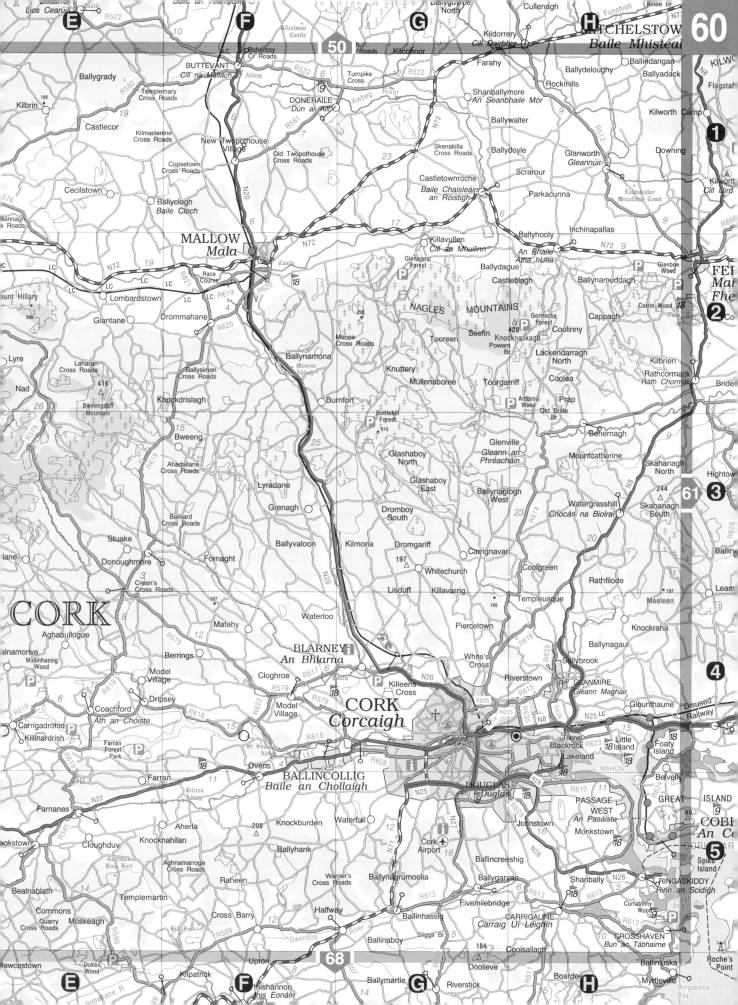

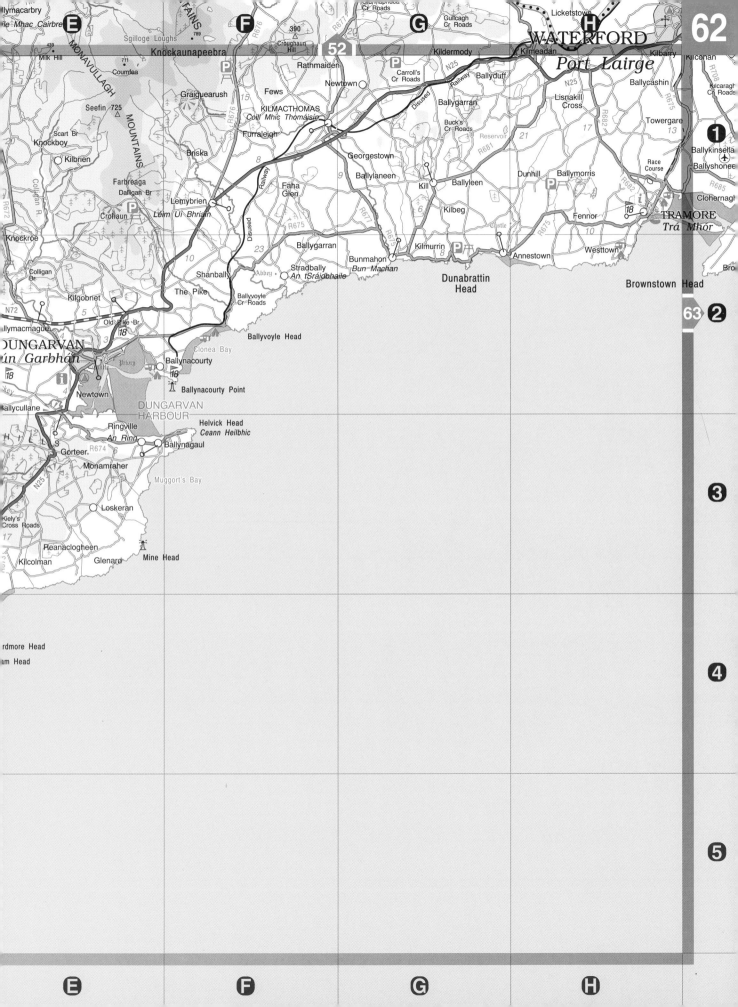

Bree
Ballylucas
E
F
G
H

Oilgate
151
Maolán na
nGabhar
Ballyhoge
Redgate
Screen
14

Galbally
Tinnakilla
N11
9
Curracloe
WEXFORD
or
NORTH BAY
1
Ballinclay
Killurin
Crossabeg
Castlebridge
Droichead An
Chaisleáin
Glynn
126
Blackhall
The Raven Point
aghmon
ach Munna
Colestown
WEXFORD
Loch Garman
Rosslare Point
Race
Course
Aughfad
Forth
Mountain
235
Clonard
Great
Kerloge
Drinagh
2
Murntown
N25
ROSSLARE
or
SOUTH BAY
Tullycanna
Cleristown
Heavenstown
Piercetown
18
Knocktown
Cr Roads
Mayglass
Killinick
R740
Ballycogly
Horetown
ROSSLARE
Ros Láir
N25
Car Ferry
ROSSLARE HARBOUR
Calafort Ros Láir
53
Bridgetown
Baile an Droichid
Hilltown
R736
Twelveacre
Cr Roads
Tagoat
Kilrane
18
Greenore Point
54
Fishguard (V)
Pembroke (V)

Duncormick
Tenacre
Cr Roads
Broadway
Lady's
Island
Ballare
Cherbourg (V)
Roscoff (V)

Park
Tomhaggard
Tacumshane
Windmill
Lady's
Island
Lake
Tuskar
Rock
3
Killag
Grange
Kilmore
Tacumshane
Lake
Ring
Churchtown
BALLYTEIGE
BAY
Newtown
Bastardstown

Kilmore
Quay
CARNSORE POINT
Ceann an Chairn
Crossfarnoge
or Forlorn Point

4
Saltee Islands

5

Little Skellig

Great Skellig   Skellig Michael

BOLUS HEAD

Hog's Head

BAY

Coomakesta Pass

Cahernageeha

Mountain   Castle Cove

542

N70

Beenarourke   Caherdaniel   *Cathair Donall*

Sheehan's Point   Derrynane Nat. Park   6

Abbey Island   Ogham Stone

Derrynane Bay

❶   Deenish Island

Scariff Island   Lamb's Head

Cod's Head   11   R575

Knocknagaliau

❷   Allihies   *Na hAllichi*

Ballydonegan

Garnish Point   Garnish Bay   6

DURSEY ISLAND   Cable Car   Lackacroghan   Cahermore

Ballynacallagh   Firkeel   10

The Bull   Kilmichael   R572

The Cow   White Ball Head

DURSEY HEAD   Black Ball Hea

❸   Crow Head

The Calf

A T L A N T I C

❹

O C E A N

❺

Ballincurrig
Riesk
Rathorgan
Walshtown
Leamlara
Lisgoold
Slievecorran
Dungourney
Cloinmult
Mount Uniacke
Inch
Grange
Dangan
Kinsalebeg
Curragh
Crowbally
Glenbower Wood
Ballynacole
Ballykilty
YOUGHAL
Eochaill
Moord
Killeagh
Cill La
ARDMORE
Aird Mhór
Ardmore Head
Ram Head
Curragh Wood
MIDLETON
Mainistir an
Corann
Mogeely
Knocknaskagh
Disused
Railway
Gortaroo
Cabin Point
CARRIGTOHILL
Carraig Thuathail
N257
N25
CASTLEMARTYR
Baile na Martra
Ballymadog
Clonard
Clonard Rock
YOUGHAL BAY
Ballynacorra
Castlemartyt Wood
Garrymore
Ladysbridge
Droichead na Scuab
Ballymacoda
58
Greenland
Kilcredan
Knockadoon Head
43
98
ISLAND
Marlogue Wood
Ballymore
CLOYNE
Cluain
Cathedral
Garryvoe
COBH
An Cóbh
Rostellan Wood
Saleen
Killmacahill
Round Tower
Shanagarry
BALLYCOTTON BAY
K HARBOUR
R631
Rostellan
Ballydavid
Churchtown
BALLYCOTTON
Baile Choitin
Spike Island
R630
Aghada
88
WHITEGATE
An Geata Bán
Ardra
Ballylanders
Inch
Gyleen
Roche's Point
Trabolgan
Power Head
abella
Swansea (V)
Roscoff (V)
CELTIC SEA

N1
To BELFAST
SWORDS

N1

M50

N32

R123

Darndale

BALDOYLE

Donaghmede

R104

Kilmore
Beaumont
Hospital

R107

R106

Ireland's
Eye

SUTTON

LC

LC

LC

9 LC

9 LC

R105

HOWTH

BEAUMONT

COOLOCK

Edenmore

Kilbarrack

R105

18

18

ARTANE

RAHENY

R105

18

DONNYCARNEY

KILLESTER

18

Bull Island

18

North

DOLLYMOUNT

18

MARINO

CLONTARF

18

Fairview

R105

East Wall

Connolly
Station

R101

Dublin Harbour

To Isle of Man (V)

North Wall

River Liffey

Irish Ferries &
Isle of Man
Terminal

To Holyhead / Liverpool (V)

RINGSEND

Hosp

IRISHTOWN

LC

Hosp

SANDYMOUNT

DUBLIN BAY

BALLSBRIDGE

R.D.S.

LC

LC

Tourist Office
Tel 1850 230330
01-6057700

DONNYBROOK

MERRION

R.T.E.

LC

CLONSKEAGH

St Vincent's
Hospital

18

Hosp

To Holyhead (V)

MILTOWN

University College
Dublin

R112

N11

BOOTERSTOWN

R118

Windy
Arbour

Clinic

BLACKROCK

O Km   1   2   3   4

O Mls   ½   1   1½   2

Scale 1:69 000

Stena Ferries
Terminal

MOUNT
MERRION

N31

N31

MONKSTOWN

DÚN
LAOGHAIRE

GOATSTOWN

DUNDRUM

KILMACUD

Glasthule

STILLORGAN

DEANS GRANGE

N11
To BRAY
WICKLOW
WEXFORD

KILL OF
THE
GRANGE

DALKEY

Galloping
Green

SALLYNOGGIN

Hosp

Dalkey
Island

Redburn
Country Park

A2
BANGOR   12   7
KNOCKNAGONEY

0 Km   ¼   ½   ¾   1
0 Mls   ¼   ½
Scale 1:27 000

Stranraer
HSS
Terminal

Belfast City
Airport

Victoria
Park

SYDENHAM

HOLYWOOD ROAD

SYDENHAM-BY-PASS

PARKWAY

Belmont   Park

OLD HOLYWOOD ROAD

BELMONT ROAD

Stormont

College

NEWTOWNARDS ROAD

BELMONT   ROAD

BELMONT

A20
NEWTOWNARDS   9   6

BALLYMACARRET

Leisure
Centre

STRANDTOWN

UPPER NEWTOWNARDS ROAD

BEERSBRIDGE ROAD

NORTH ROAD

BLOOMFIELD

BALLYHACKAMORE

GRAND PARADE

KING'S   ROAD

TULLYCARNET

Greenville
Park

KNOCK

KNOCK ROAD

GILNAHIRK ROAD

College

WOODSTOCK ROAD

CASTLEREAGH ROAD

GILNAHIRK

rmeau
Park

RAVENHILL ROAD

18

College

LADAS DRIVE

CASTLEREAGH

18

BRANIEL

Colleges

MOUNT MERRION AVENUE

CREGAGH ROAD

BALLYNAFEIGH

CREGAGH

KNOCKBREDA ROAD

UPPER   BRANIEL ROAD

18

SAINFIELD ROAD

UPPER

MANSE ROAD

BALLYGOWAN ROAD

A24
BALLYNAHINCH   17   11
DOWNPATRICK   29   18
NEWCASTLE   41   26

N8
TO DUBLIN

GLANMIRE

LYVOLANE

BALLYVOLANE ROAD

Mayfield
Cross

R615

BARNAVARA

R639

Glashaboy River

Indust
Estate

MAYFIELD

Dunkettle

MONTENOTTE

TIVOLI

Lota

Hosps

NEW ROAD

R614

R635

Hosps

N8

LOWER GLANMIRE ROAD

N8

Industrial
Estate

N25
TO WATERFORD

R623

RIVER LEE

Páirc
Uí Chaoimh

BLACKROCK

Jack Lynch
Tunnel

Hosp

Hosp

BOREENMANAGH ROAD

BALLINTEMPLE

MAHON

BALLINLOUGH

Coll

Hosp

BALLINURE

DOUGLAS ROAD

Indust
Estate

R610

Douglas

N25

SOUTH DOUGLAS ROAD

Goat
Isd

Hospital

R610
TO PASSAGE WEST

BALLYPHEHANE

River

N28

ROCHESTOWN ROAD

N25

R610

Douglas

R610

ROCHESTOWN

GRANGE

CARRIG HILL

N28

DONNYBROOK

Sch

N28
TO RINGASKIDDY
AND FERRY

KILKENNY

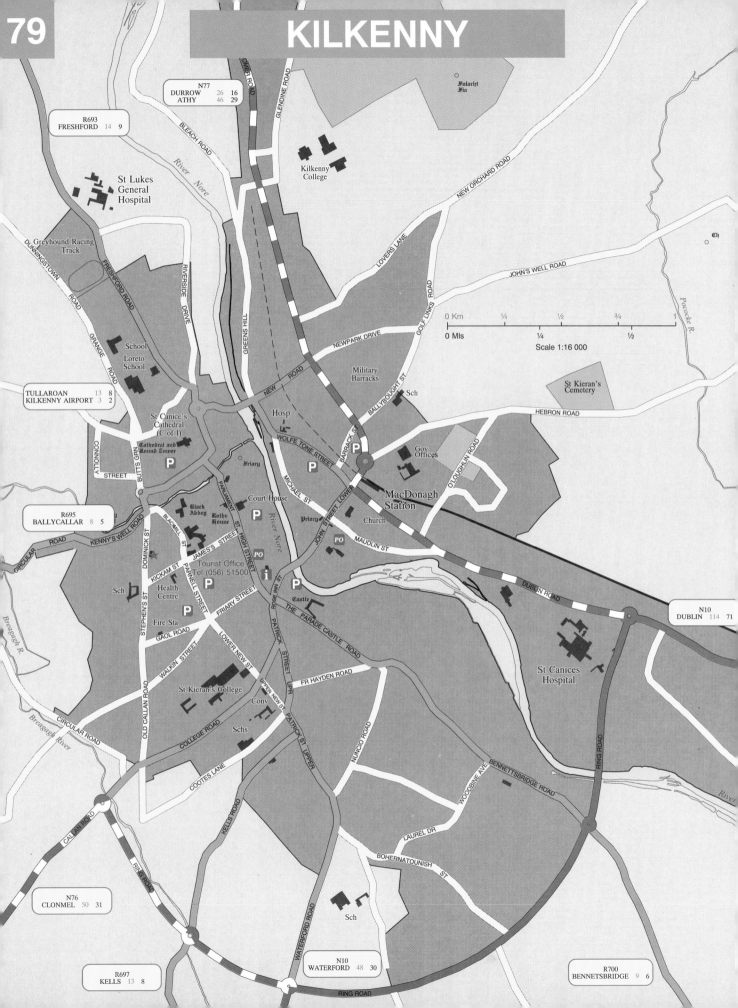

N77
DURROW 26 16
ATHY 46 29

R693
FRESHFORD 14 9

Fulacht
Fia

BLEACH ROAD

River Nore

Kilkenny
College

St Lukes
General
Hospital

NEW ORCHARD ROAD

Ch

Greyhound Racing
Track

DUNNINGSTOWN ROAD

FRESHFORD ROAD

RIVERSIDE DRIVE

GREENS HILL

OMER ROAD

GLENDINE ROAD

Lovers Lane

GOLF LINKS ROAD

JOHN'S WELL ROAD

Pococke R.

School
Loreto
School

GRANGE ROAD

NEW ROAD

NEWPARK DRIVE

Military
Barracks

BALLYBOUGHT ST

Sch

0 Km   ¼   ½   ¾   1
0 Mls   ¼   ½
Scale 1:16 000

St Kieran's
Cemetery

HEBRON ROAD

TULLAROAN 13 8
KILKENNY AIRPORT 3 2

St Canice's
Cathedral
(C of I)

Hosp

WOLFE TONE STREET

BARRACK ST

P

Gov
Offices

O'LOUGHLIN ROAD

CONNOLLY STREET

Cathedral and
Round Tower

BUTTS GRN

P

Friary

MICHAEL ST

P

MacDonagh
Station

R695
BALLYCALLAR 8 5

KENNY'S WELL ROAD

CIRCULAR ROAD

Breagagh R.

DOMINICK ST

BLACKMILL ST

Black Abbey

PARLIAMENT ST

Rothe House

Court House

JAMES'S STREET

HIGH STREET

P

Priory

JOHN STREET LOWER

PO

Church

MAUDLIN ST

DUBLIN ROAD

N10
DUBLIN 114 71

Sch

STEPHEN'S ST

KICKAM ST

PARNELL STREET

Health
Centre

P

Fire Sta

Gaol Road

PO

Tourist Office
Tel (056) 51500

i

P

Castle

ROSE INN ST

THE PARADE

CASTLE ROAD

St Canices
Hospital

WALKIN STREET

OLD CALLAN ROAD

LOWER NEW ST

Friary Street

St Kieran's College

UPPER NEW ST

Conv

Schs

PATRICK STREET

PATRICK ST UPPER

FR HAYDEN ROAD

NUNCIO ROAD

COLLEGE ROAD

COOTES LANE

KELLS ROAD

WATERFORD ROAD

WOODBINE AVE

BENNETTSBRIDGE ROAD

RING ROAD

CIRCULAR ROAD

Breagagh River

CALLAN ROAD

RING ROAD

LAUREL DR

BOHERNATOUNISH ST

River

N76
CLONMEL 50 31

Sch

R697
KELLS 13 8

N10
WATERFORD 48 30

RING ROAD

R700
BENNETTSBRIDGE 9 6

WATERFORD

N 25		
NEW ROSS	24	15
WEXFORD	61	38

Belmount Park Hospital

RIVER SUIR

Waterpark (R.F.C.)

Hospital

Sch

MAYPARK LANE

NURSERY LANE

Scale 1:23 000

DUNMORE ROAD

Golf Course

Plunket Station (Bus and Rail)

Sch

ABBEY ROAD

DOCK ROAD

Church

NEWTOWN ROAD

People's Park

Sch

Schs

St Patrick's Hospital

UPPER GRANGE ROAD

St Otteran's Hospital

Sch

PASSAGE ROAD

LWR NEWTOWN

JOHN'S HILL

Fire Sta

LOMBARD ST

PARADE ST

CATHERINE ST

ST

G.P.O.

I.G.P.O.

P Tourist Office
Tel (051)875823

P

LADY LA

THE MALL

CUSTOM HS QY

COAL QY

MERCHANTS QY

MICHAEL ST

JOHN STREET

RICHARDSON'S LA

St John's College

PO

BALLYTRUCKLE ROAD

Greyhound Racing Track

Sch

St

BATH ST

Gaelic Park

Conv Sch

Sch

Rice Bridge

GRATTAN QUAY

THOMAS ST

MORGAN STREET

BARRACK STREET

CASTLE ST

MANOR STREET

COLLEGE STREET

Sch

Holy Ghost Hospital

John's RIVER

RING ROAD

CORK ROAD

INNER RING ROAD

TRAMORE ROAD

SUMMER HILL BRIDGE

LOWER YELLOW ROAD

Newport's Sq

DOYLE'S ST

MORRISSONS RD

HENNESSY'S RD

CANNON STREET

Ch

Sch

PO

Kilbarry Cr Rds

Bleach Bridge

LACKEN ROAD

GRACEDIEU ROAD

Airmount Hospital

Schs

PO

BILBERRY ROAD

NEWRATH ROAD

KEANE'S ROAD

CLEABOY ROAD

SKIBBEREEN ROAD

WHITE ROAD

Ch Sch

Sch

Instute of Technology

BROWNS ROAD

College

TIRCONNELL AVE

KILBARRY ROAD

Sch Church

N 9		
DUBLIN	163	101
LIMERICK	129	80

N25		
CORK	126	78
KILLARNEY	193	120

R675
TRAMORE 12 7

R708
AIRPORT 9 6

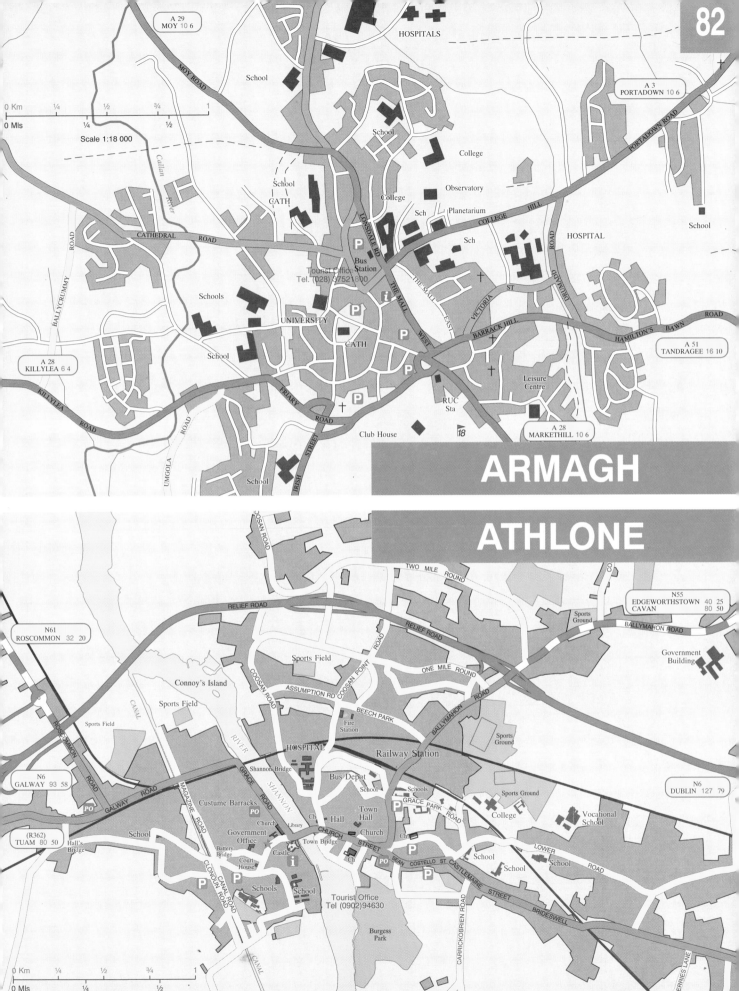

ARMAGH

ATHLONE

ARMAGH map labels:

A 29
MOY 10 6

A 3
PORTADOWN 10 6

HOSPITALS

School

MOY ROAD

PORTADOWN ROAD

School

College

Callan River

Observatory

School

GATH

Planetarium

College

Sch

COLLEGE HILL

School

CATHEDRAL ROAD

Sch

HOSPITAL

DRUMGOR

BALLYCRUMMY ROAD

LONSDALE RD

P

Bus Station

Tourist Office
Tel. (028) 37521800

i

THE MALL EAST

VICTORIA ST

HAMILTON'S BAWN ROAD

Schools

P

THE MALL WEST

BARRACK HILL

A 51
TANDRAGEE 16 10

UNIVERSITY

P

P

A 28
KILLYLEA 6 4

School

CATH

KILLYLEA ROAD

School

P

Leisure Centre

FRIARY ROAD

UMGOLA ROAD

IRISH STREET

P

RUC Sta

18

A 28
MARKETHILL 10 6

Club House

School

Scale 1:18 000

ATHLONE map labels:

COOSAN ROAD

TWO MILE ROUND

N55
EDGEWORTHSTOWN 40 25
CAVAN 80 50

RELIEF ROAD

Sports Ground

BALLYMAHON ROAD

N61
ROSCOMMON 32 20

RELIEF ROAD

ONE MILE ROUND

Government Building

Sports Field

Connoy's Island

COOSAN ROAD

COOSAN POINT ROAD

ASSUMPTION RD

Sports Field

BEECH PARK

BALLYMAHON ROAD

Sports Field

Sports Ground

Fire Station

CANAL

RIVER SHANNON

HOSPITAL

Railway Station

N6
GALWAY 93 58

ROSCOMMON ROAD

Shannon Bridge

Bus Depot

School

Schools

Sports Ground

PO

MAGAZINE ROAD

Custume Barracks

PO

School

GRACE PARK ROAD

College

Vocational School

(R362)
TUAM 80 50

GALWAY ROAD

Church

Library

Town Hall

P

GRACE PARK ROAD

N6
DUBLIN 127 79

School

Government Office

Church

Ch

LOWER ROAD

Hall's Bridge

Battery Bridge

Town Bridge

CHURCH STREET

PO

P

School

School

Castle

i

Ch

SEAN COSTELLO ST

CASTLEMAINE STREET

CLONOWN ROAD

P

Court House

School

P

School

CANAL ROAD

Schools

Tourist Office
Tel (0902)94630

CARRICKOBRIEN ROAD

BRIDESWELL

DERRIES LANE

Burgess Park

CANAL

Scale 1:20 000

BALLYMENA

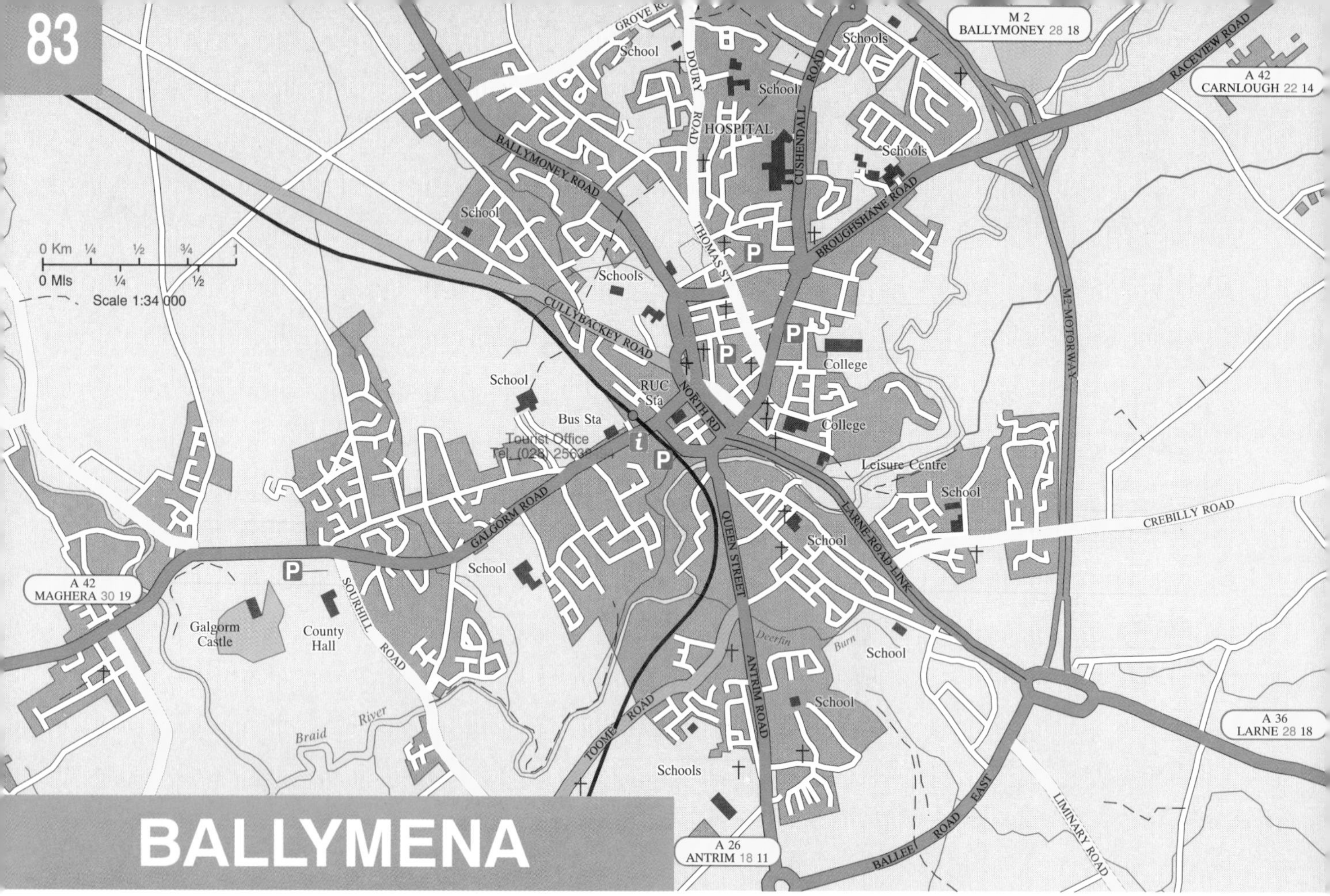
M 2
BALLYMONEY 28 18
A 42
CARNLOUGH 22 14
A 42
MAGHERA 30 19
A 26
ANTRIM 18 11
A 36
LARNE 28 18
0 Km ¼ ½ ¾ 1
0 Mls ¼ ½
Scale 1:34 000
GROVE RD
DOURY ROAD
CUSHENDALL ROAD
BALLYMONEY ROAD
BROUGHSHANE ROAD
RACEVIEW ROAD
THOMAS ST
CULLYBACKEY ROAD
NORTH RD
GALGORM ROAD
QUEEN STREET
LARNE ROAD LINK
CREBILLY ROAD
M2 MOTORWAY
SOURHILL ROAD
ANTRIM ROAD
TOOME ROAD
BALLEE ROAD EAST
LIMINARY ROAD
HOSPITAL
Schools
School
College
Leisure Centre
RUC Sta
Bus Sta
Tourist Office
Galgorm Castle
County Hall
Braid River
Deerfin Burn

BANGOR

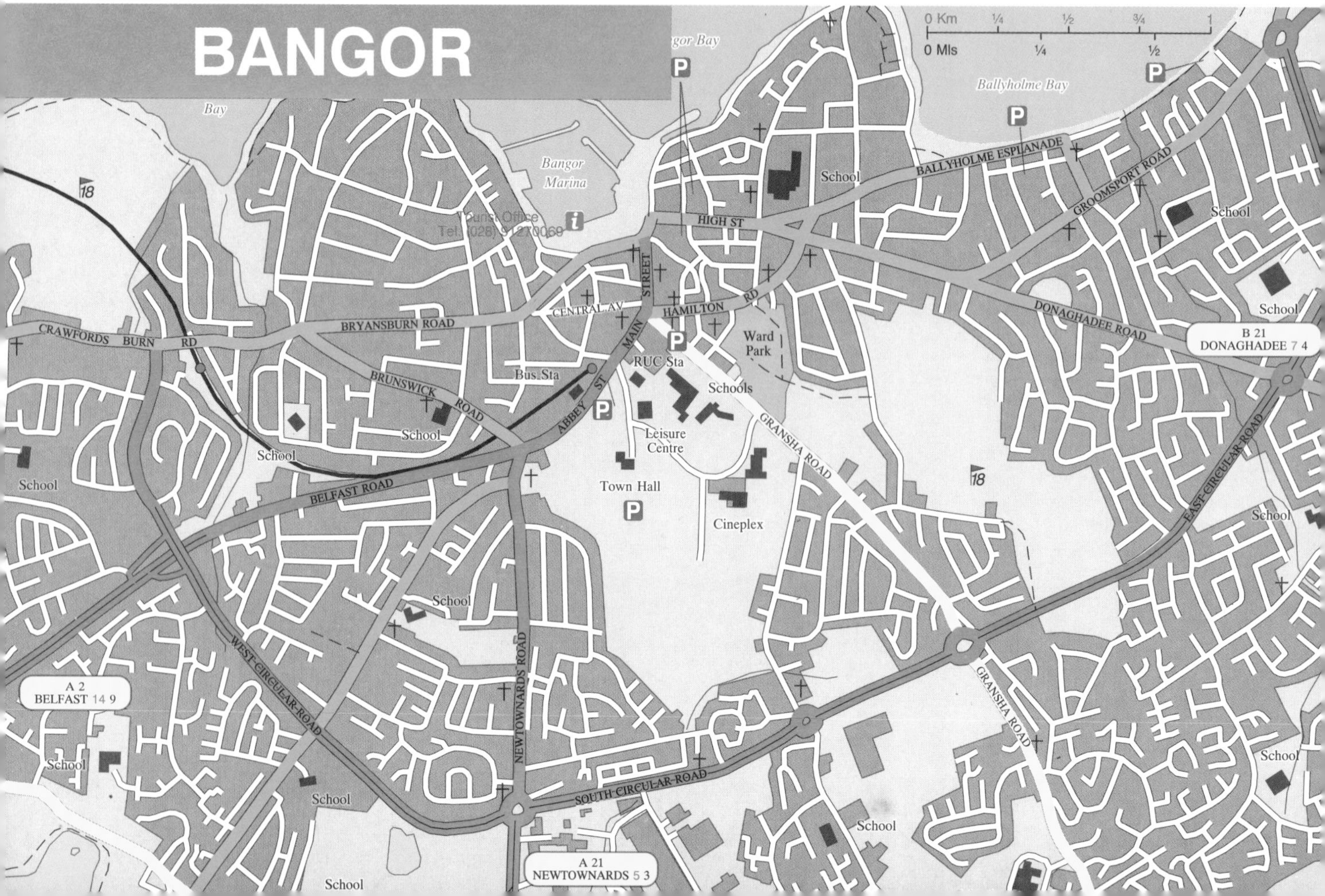
0 Km ¼ ½ ¾ 1
0 Mls ¼ ½
Bangor Bay
Ballyholme Bay
Bangor Marina
Tourist Office
Tel. (028) 91270069
HIGH ST
BALLYHOLME ESPLANADE
GROOMSPORT ROAD
DONAGHADEE ROAD
CRAWFORDS BURN RD
BRYANSBURN ROAD
CENTRAL AV
HAMILTON RD
MAIN STREET
ABBEY ST
BRUNSWICK ROAD
BELFAST ROAD
GRANSHA ROAD
EAST CIRCULAR ROAD
WEST CIRCULAR ROAD
NEWTOWNARDS ROAD
SOUTH CIRCULAR ROAD
B 21
DONAGHADEE 7 4
A 2
BELFAST 14 9
A 21
NEWTOWNARDS 5 3
Ward Park
RUC Sta
Bus Sta
Schools
School
Leisure Centre
Town Hall
Cineplex

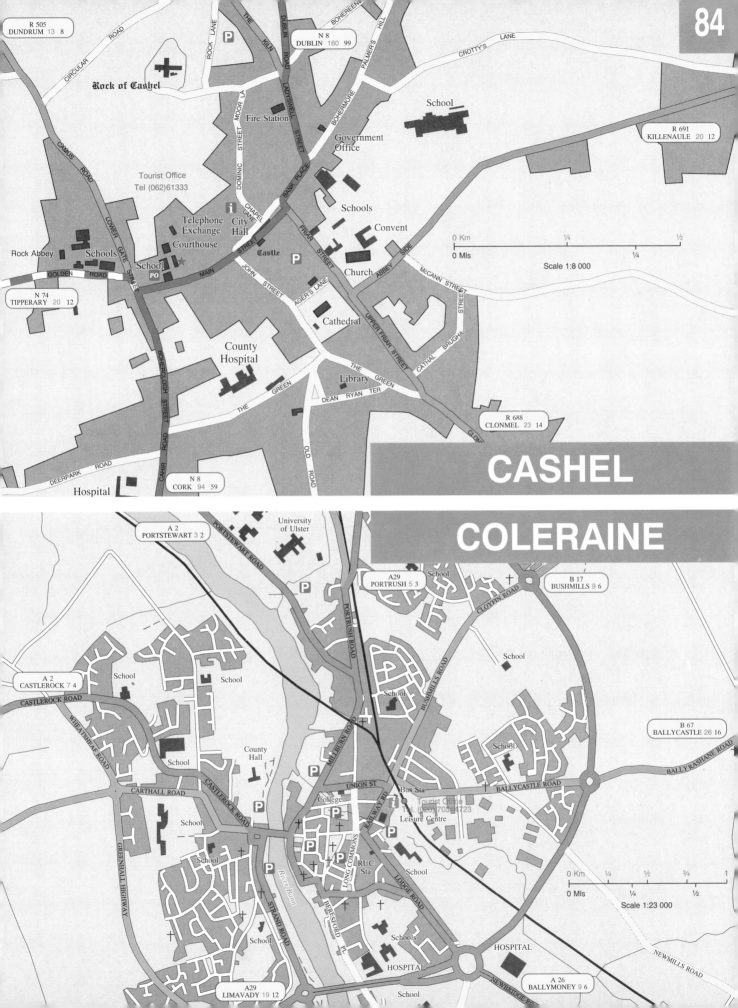

CASHEL

COLERAINE

R 505
DUNDRUM 13 8

N 8
DUBLIN 160 99

R 691
KILLENAULE 20 12

Rock of Cashel

Rock Lane

THE

KILN ROAD

DUBLIN ROAD

BOHEREEN

PALMER'S HILL

CROTTY'S LANE

CIRCULAR ROAD

Fire Station

School

CAMUS ROAD

DOMINIC STREET

MOOR LANE

LADYSWELL STREET

Government Office

Tourist Office
Tel (062)61333

Telephone Exchange

CHAPEL LANE

City Hall

Courthouse

BANK PLACE

Schools

Convent

0 Km   ¼   ½
0 Mls   ¼
Scale 1:8 000

Rock Abbey

Schools

School

PO

GOLDEN ROAD

LOWER GATE STREET

Castle

STREET

Church

FRIAR STREET

ABBEY SIDE

McCANN STREET

STREET

N 74
TIPPERARY 20 12

MAIN

JOHN STREET

AGER'S LANE

Cathedral

UPPER FRIAR STREET

CATHAL BRUGHA

BOHERCLOGH STREET

County Hospital

THE GREEN

Library

THE GREEN

DEAN RYAN TER

R 688
CLONMEL 23 14

CAHIR ROAD

OLD ROAD

CLONM

DEERPARK ROAD

Hospital

N 8
CORK 94 59

A 2
PORTSTEWART 3 2

University of Ulster

PORTSTEWART ROAD

A29
PORTRUSH 5 3

School

CLOYFIN ROAD

B 17
BUSHMILLS 9 6

PORTRUSH ROAD

School

A 2
CASTLEROCK 7 4

School

School

BUSHMILLS ROAD

School

CASTLEROCK ROAD

School

WHEATSHEAF ROAD

MILBURN ROAD

School

B 67
BALLYCASTLE 26 16

County Hall

BALLY RASHANE ROAD

GREENHALL HIGHWAY

School

CASTLEROCK ROAD

UNION ST

Bus Sta

BALLYCASTLE ROAD

CARTHALL ROAD

College

Tourist Office
Tel. (028)70354723

Leisure Centre

School

0 Km   ¼   ½   ¾   1
0 Mls   ¼   ½
Scale 1:23 000

School

RAILWAY RD

School

LONG COMMONS

RUC Sta

LODGE ROAD

River Bann

STRAND ROAD

BERESFORD

Schools

HOSPITAL

A29
LIMAVADY 19 12

HOSPITAL

NEWBRIDGE RD

A 26
BALLYMONEY 9 6

NEWMILLS ROAD

School

85

CRAIGAVON - LURGAN

CRAIGAVON - PORTADOWN

Map 1 (Craigavon – Lurgan) labels:

School
A 76/M 1 BELFAST 37 23
School
18
SILVERWOOD ROAD
School
RUC Sta
FRANCES STREET
Schools
NORTH STREET
i
P
EAST WAY
Schools
School
18
A 3 MOIRA 5 3
P
School
AVENUE ROAD
School
P
PORTADOWN ROAD
Leisure Complex
UNION STREET
HOSPITAL
BANBRIDGE ROAD
A 3 PORTADOWN 2 1
Tourist Office Tel. (028) 38322205
LAKE ROAD
OLD PORTADOWN ROAD
School
Civic Centre
RUC Sta
i
School
P
CENTRAL WAY
P
Schools
P
Court House
DRUMGOR ROAD
Schools
BROWNLOW ROAD
GILFORD ROAD
A 26 BANBRIDGE 9 6
School
Leisure Centre
P
School
MONBRIEF EAST ROAD
0 Km ¼ ½ ¾ 1
0 Mls ¼ ½
Scale 1:29 000

Map 2 (Craigavon – Portadown) labels:

B 2/M 1 BELFAST 45 28
A 27 LURGAN 4 2
A 4/M 1 DUNGANNON 22 14
School
HOSPITAL
DUNGANNON ROAD
DERRYANVIL ROAD
School
LURGAN ROAD
SEAGOE ROAD
School
MOY ROAD
School
NORTHWAY
OLD LURGAN ROAD
CORCULLENTRAGH ROAD
GARVAGHY ROAD
School
College
School
School
P
BRIDGE STREET
KILLYCOMAIN ROAD
CORCRAIN ROAD
MARKET ST
P
School
LOUGHGALL ROAD
P
RUC Sta
School
NORTHWAY
P
i
Swimming Pool
GILFORD ROAD
Tourist Office Tel. (028) 38332802
School
THOMAS ROAD
School
BROWNSTOWN ROAD
ARMAGH ROAD
River Bann
DRUMNACANVY ROAD
TANDRAGEE ROAD
A 3 ARMAGH 14 9
A 50 BANBRIDGE 14 8
Scale 1:28 000
0 Km ¼ ½ ¾
0 Mls ¼ ½

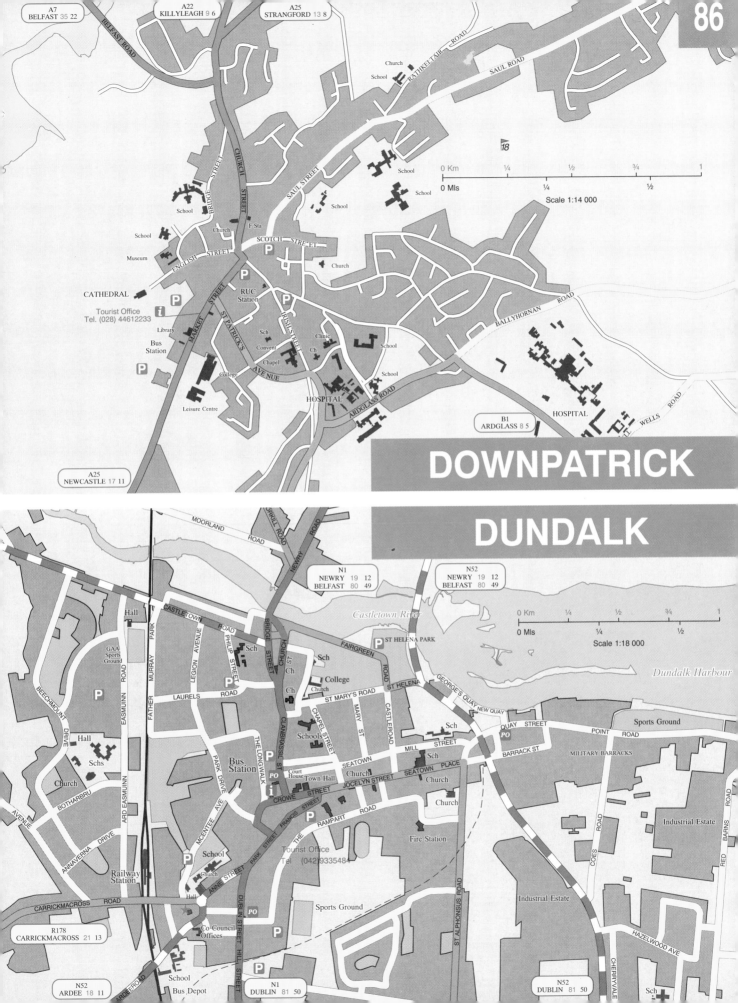

DOWNPATRICK

DUNDALK

A7
BELFAST 35 22

A22
KILLYLEAGH 9 6

A25
STRANGFORD 13 8

RATHKELTAIR ROAD

SAUL ROAD

Church

School

School

BELFAST ROAD

BRIDGE STREET

CHURCH STREET

SAUL STREET

School

School

School

School

School

Church

F Sta

SCOTCH STREET

Church

ENGLISH STREET

Museum

P

Church

Church

CATHEDRAL

RUC Station

P

Tourist Office
Tel. (028) 44612233
i

P

Library

MARKET STREET

ST PATRICK'S

Sch

Clinic

Ch

School

BALLYHORNAN ROAD

Bus Station

IRISH STREET

Conveni

Ch

School

HOSPITAL

Chapel

P

AVENUE

College

School

Leisure Centre

ARDGLASS ROAD

HOSPITAL

WELLS ROAD

B1
ARDGLASS 8 5

A25
NEWCASTLE 17 11

0 Km   ¼   ½   ¾   1
0 Mls   ¼   ½
Scale 1:14 000

i18

MOORLAND ROAD

ORKILL ROAD

NEWRY ROAD

Castletown River

N1
NEWRY 19 12
BELFAST 80 49

N52
NEWRY 19 12
BELFAST 80 49

0 Km   ¼   ½   ¾   1
0 Mls   ¼   ½
Scale 1:18 000

Dundalk Harbour

Hall

CASTLETOWN ROAD

PARK

MURRAY

PHILIP STREET

Sch

BRIDGE STREET

CHURCH ST

Ch

Sch

FAIRGREEN

P

St Helena Park

GAA Sports Ground

LEGION AVENUE

Ch

College

Church

ST MARY'S ROAD

ST HELENA

GEORGE'S QUAY

NEW QUAY

EASMUINN ROAD

P

LAURELS ROAD

MARY ST

CASTLEROAD

Sports Ground

BEECHMOUNT DRIVE

FATHER

CHAPEL STREET

Schools

Sch

QUAY STREET

PO

POINT ROAD

Hall

ARD EASMUINN

PARK DRIVE

THE LONGWALK

Bus Station

CLANBRASSIL ST

SEATOWN

MILL STREET

Sch

BARRACK ST

MILITARY BARRACKS

Schs

PO

Court House

Town Hall

JOCELYN STREET

SEATOWN PLACE

Church

COES ROAD

Church

Church

i

CROWE STREET

RAMPART ROAD

Industrial Estate

BOTHARBRU

MCENTEE AVE

THE

FRANCIS STREET

Church

P

ANNAVERNA DRIVE

AVENUE

School

Tourist Office
Tel (042)9335484

Fire Station

RED BARNS ROAD

ANNE STREET

Church

PARK STREET

DUBLIN STREET

PO

Industrial Estate

Railway Station

Hall

P

Sports Ground

HAZELWOOD AVE

CARRICKMACROSS ROAD

R178
CARRICKMACROSS 21 13

Co Council Offices

HILL STREET

ST ALPHONSUS ROAD

CHERRYVALE

N52
ARDEE 18 11

School

Bus Depot

ARDEE ROAD

N1
DUBLIN 81 50

P

N52
DUBLIN 81 50

Sch

ENNISKILLEN

KILLARNEY

Scale 1:18 000

0 Km   ¼   ½   ¾

0 Mls   ¼   ½

A 46
BELLEEK 35 22

A 32
IRVINESTOWN 14 8

Lough Erne

Back Lough

Race Course
Lough

CORNAGRADE ROAD

IRVINESTOWN ROAD

School

School

School

Cinema

School

School

School

School

HOSPITAL

DERRYGONNELLY ROAD

School

School

ROSSORRY

CHURCH ROAD

THE BROOK

HENRY STREET

RUC Sta

QUEEN ST

CATH

School

School

School

FORTHILL ST

TEMPO ROAD

P

P

P

P

i
Tourist Office
Tel. (028) 66323110

WELLINGTON ROAD

Post
Office

Lakeland
Forum

Bus
Depot

P

College

School

School

DUBLIN ROAD

P

Upper Lough Erne

Rossole Lough

School

18

A 4
LISBELLAW 5 3

N22
TRALEE 31 19
LIMERICK 111 69

0 Km   ¼   ½   ¾   1

0 Mls   ¼   ½

Scale 1:19 000

N72
RING OF KERRY
KILLORGLIN 21 13

St Finan's
Hospital

Convent

ST MARGARET'S ROAD

ROCK ROAD

Fitzgerald Stadium

NORTH RING ROAD

Fire
Station

Government
Buildings

UPPER PARK ROAD

KNOCKREER

District
Hospital

PORT ROAD

Deenagh River

Convent
School

School

NEW ROAD

College

Convent

Cathedral

CATHEDRAL PL

BOHEREEN-NA-GOUN

HIGH STREET

School

NEW STREET

Library

ST ANNE'S ROAD

EMMET ROAD

P

Hall

Church

Courthouse

FAIR
HILL

Br. Ht.
4.75m

PARK   ROAD

Church

N22
CORK 86 54
MACROOM 48 30
MALLOW 66 41
DUBLIN 304 189

MAIN ST

COLLEGE ST

ST AVE RD

P

P

Church

Town Hall

Bus Depot

Railway
Station

PO

P

i

Tourist Office
Tel (064)31633

Church

COUNTESS ROAD

COTTER'S FARM

P

ROSS   ROAD

FLESK ROAD

MUCKROSS ROAD

WOODLAWN ROAD

School

BALLYCASHEEN ROAD

MILL ROAD

River Flesk

KILLARNEY
NATIONAL PARK

N71
MUCKROSS HOUSE 6 4
RING OF KERRY
KENMARE 32 20
BANTRY 78 49

Race Course

River Flesk

DROMHUMPER

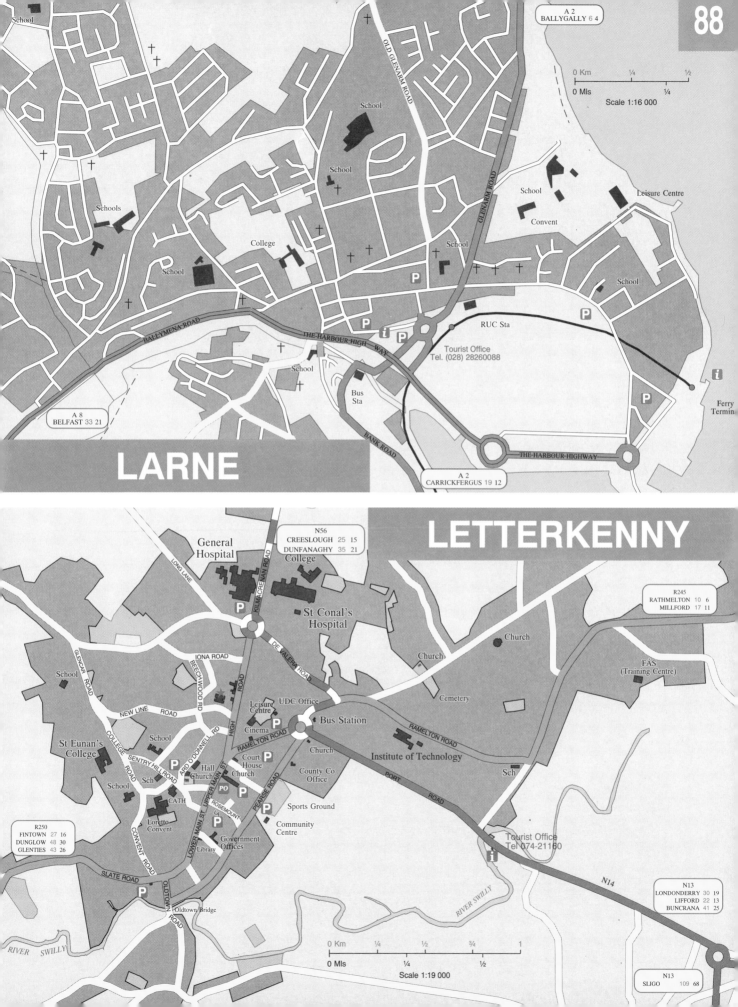

LARNE

LETTERKENNY

LARNE

School

School

School

School

School

Schools

College

School

School

School

School

Convent

Leisure Centre

School

School

BALLYMENA ROAD

THE HARBOUR HIGH WAY

OLD GLENARM ROAD

GLENARM ROAD

RUC Sta

Tourist Office
Tel. (028) 28260088

Bus
Sta

BANK ROAD

THE HARBOUR HIGHWAY

A 2		
BALLYGALLY	6	4

A 8		
BELFAST	33	21

A 2		
CARRICKFERGUS	19	12

Ferry Terminal

0 Km   ¼   ½
0 Mls   ¼
Scale 1:16 000

LETTERKENNY

General
Hospital

College

St Conal's
Hospital

Church

Church

Church

Cemetery

FÁS
(Training Centre)

School

IONA ROAD

BEECHWOOD RD

GLENCAR ROAD

NEW LINE ROAD

St Eunan's
College

COLLEGE ROAD

SENTRY HILL ROAD

School

School

Sch

Hall
Church

CATH

Loretto
Convent

Library

CONVENT ROAD

SLATE ROAD

OLDTOWN ROAD

Oldtown Bridge

LONG LANE

KILMACRENAN ROAD

DE VALERA ROAD

HIGH ROAD

ARDO'DONNELL RD

LOWER MAIN ST UPPER MAIN ST

ROSEMOUNT

PEARSE ROAD

Leisure
Centre

Cinema

UDC Office

Bus Station

Court
House
Church

Church

County Co
Office

Sports Ground

Community
Centre

Government
Offices

PO

RAMELTON ROAD

RAMELTON ROAD

Institute of Technology

Sch

PORT ROAD

Tourist Office
Tel 074-21160

RIVER SWILLY

RIVER SWILLY

N14

N56		
CREESLOUGH	25	15
DUNFANAGHY	35	21

R245		
RATHMELTON	10	6
MILLFORD	17	11

R250		
FINTOWN	27	16
DUNGLOW	48	30
GLENTIES	43	26

N13		
LONDONDERRY	30	19
LIFFORD	22	13
BUNCRANA	41	25

N13		
SLIGO	109	68

0 Km   ¼   ½   ¾   1
0 Mls   ¼   ½
Scale 1:19 000

LISBURN

School

School

KNOCKMORE ROAD

PRINCE WILLIAM ROAD

MAGHERALAVE ROAD

School

School

Schools

Wallace Park
Tourist Office
Tel. (028) 92660038

A1
BELFAST 11 7

BALLINDERRY ROAD

WALLACE AV

Schs

CASTLE

School

CATH

i

Schools

LONGSTONE ST

GOVERNOR'S RD

Bus Sta

BRIDGE ST

QUEEN'S RD

School

School

MOIRA ROAD

School

School

RUC Sta

LAGANBANK ROAD

P

SAINTFIELD ROAD

School

HILLHALL ROAD

School

BALLYNAHINCH RD

School

Leisure Centre

School

Schools

HOSPITAL

0 Km ¼ ½ ¾ 1

0 Mls ¼ ½

Scale 1:22 000

A3
MOIRA 8 5

HILLSBOROUGH OLD ROAD

M E MOTORWAY

A49
SAINTFIELD 12
BALLYNAHINCH 14

River Lagan

Sprucefield

M1
DUNGANNON 48 30

MULLINGAR

Hospital

GREEN ROAD

LONGFORD ROAD

(N4)
LONGFORD 43 27
SLIGO 132 82

River Brosna

ROYAL CANAL

DELVIN ROAD

N52
DUNDALK 91 5

College

HARBOUR STREET

Schools

Cusack Park GAA

MILL ROAD

Sch

Cathedral

Conv

Church

COLUMB BARRACKS

Enterprise Centre

Health Centre

BISHOP'S GATE STREET

CASTLE ST

FRIARS

Church (Pres)

P

P

Church

i

Tourist Office
Tel (044)48650

County Library

COLLEGE ST

PEARSE STREET

AUSTIN FRIARS STREET

BELLVIEW ROAD

PO

P

Library

PO

Church (C of I)

DOMINICK ST

OLIVER PLUNKETT ST

MOUNT ST

School

Court House

MILLMOUNT ROAD

School

(N4)
DUBLIN 87 54

R390
ATHLONE 47 29

PATRICK STREET

P

Railway Station

Telephone Exchange

County Hall

SUNDAY WELL ROAD

Hall

ROYAL CANAL

Fire Station

CLONMORE ROAD

Greyhound Racing Track

P

0 Km ¼ ½

0 Mls ¼

Scale 1:15 000

NEWBROOK ROAD

River Brosna

LYNN ROAD

BALLINDERRY ROAD

ARDMORE ROAD

ROYAL CANAL

N52
TYRRELLSPASS 17 10
TULLAMORE 36 22

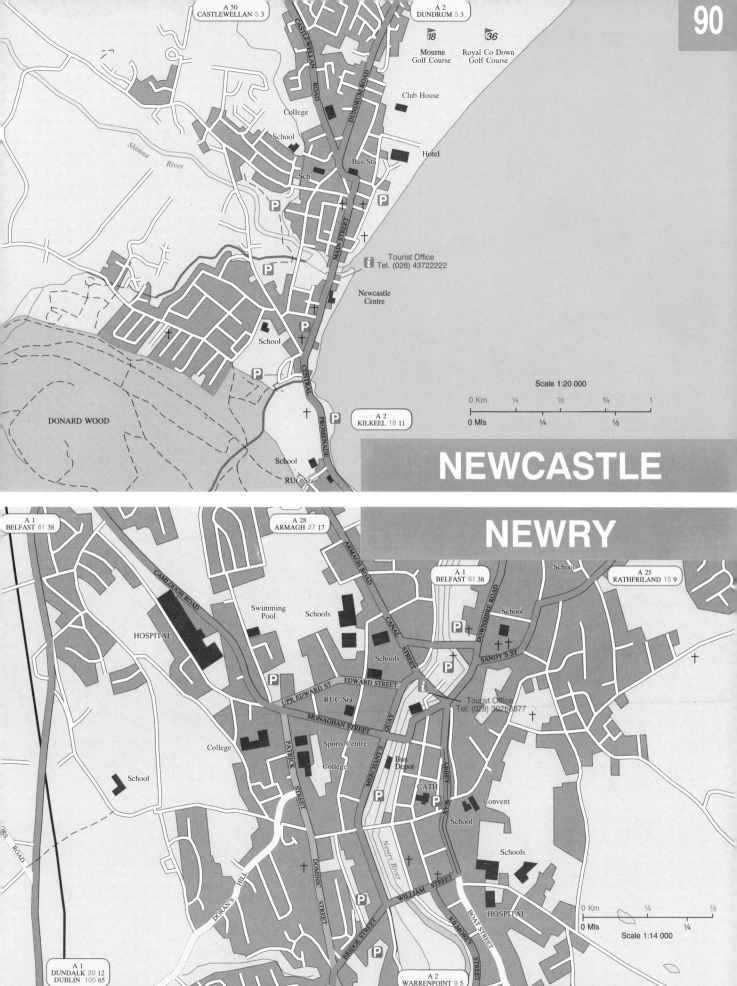

NEWCASTLE

A 50
CASTLEWELLAN 5 3

A 2
DUNDRUM 5 3

18 Mourne
Golf Course

36 Royal Co Down
Golf Course

Club House

College

School

Hotel

Bus Sta

Sch

P

P

CASTLEWELLAN ROAD

DUNDRUM ROAD

MAIN STREET

Shimna River

Tourist Office
Tel. (028) 43722222

Newcastle
Centre

P

P

School

P

CENTRAL PROMENADE

P

DONARD WOOD

A 2
KILKEEL 18 11

School

RUC Sta

Scale 1:20 000

0 Km   ¼   ½   ¾   1

0 Mls   ¼   ½

NEWRY

A 1
BELFAST 61 38

A 28
ARMAGH 27 17

A 1
BELFAST 61 38

School

A 25
RATHFRILAND 15 9

CAMLOUGH ROAD

ARMAGH ROAD

HOSPITAL

Swimming
Pool

Schools

Schools

CANAL STREET

DOWNSHIRE ROAD

School

P

SANDY'S ST

P

EDWARD STREET

UPR EDWARD ST

RUC Sta

i

Tourist Office
Tel. (028) 30268877

P

MONAGHAN STREET

College

Sports Centre

College

MERCHANT'S QUAY

Bus
Depot

PATRICK STREET

CATH

P

Convent

School

DORAN'S HILL

DOMINIC STREET

Newry River

School

Schools

ORS ROAD

P

BRIDGE STREET

WILLIAM STREET

KILMOREY STREET

BOAT STREET

ABBEY WAY

HOSPITAL

P

0 Km   ¼   ½

0 Mls   ¼

Scale 1:14 000

A 1
DUNDALK 20 12
DUBLIN 105 65

A 2
WARRENPOINT 9 5

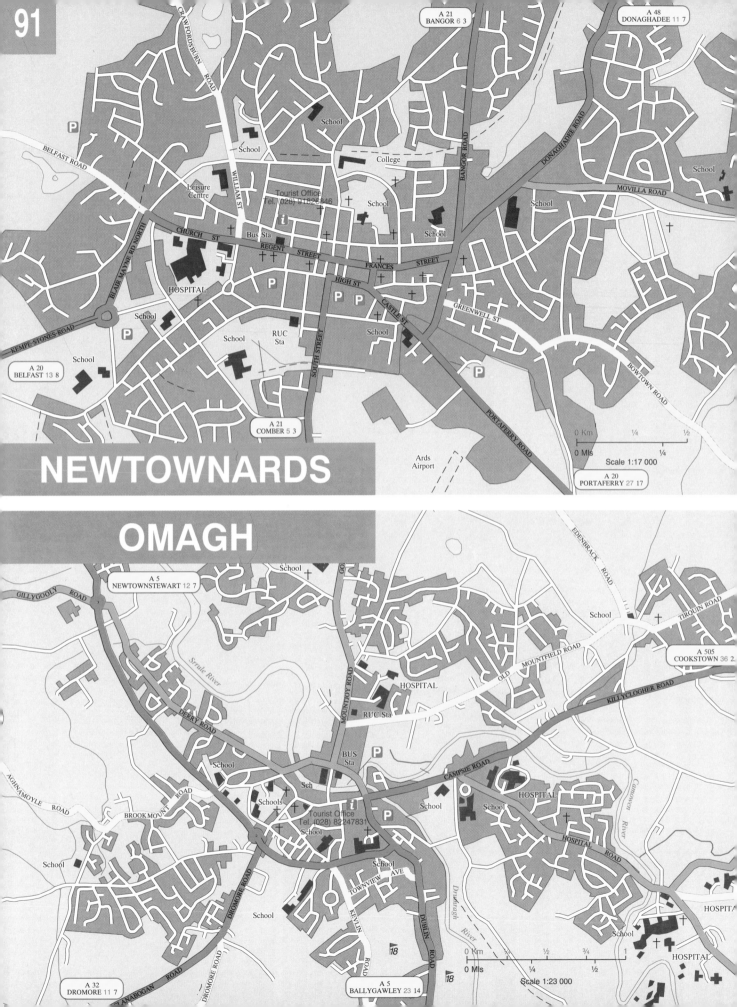

NEWTOWNARDS

OMAGH

A 21
BANGOR 6 3

A 48
DONAGHADEE 11 7

CRAWFORDSBURN ROAD

BELFAST ROAD

School

School

College

DONAGHADEE ROAD

BANGOR ROAD

School

MOVILLA ROAD

School

School

WILLIAM ST

Leisure
Centre

Tourist Office
Tel. (028) 91826846

i

School

School

CHURCH ST

REGENT STREET

FRANCES STREET

Bus Sta

BLAIR MAYNE RD NORTH

HIGH ST

P

P

P

HOSPITAL

School

GREENWELL ST

CASTLE ST

School

School

RUC
Sta

SOUTH STREET

School

School

P

School

KEMPE STONES ROAD

P

BOWTOWN ROAD

PORTAFERRY ROAD

A 20
BELFAST 13 8

A 21
COMBER 5 3

Ards
Airport

0 Km   ¼   ½
0 Mls   ¼
Scale 1:17 000

A 20
PORTAFERRY 27 17

EDENBRACK ROAD

A 5
NEWTOWNSTEWART 12 7

School

TIRQUIN ROAD

GILLYGOOLY ROAD

School

OLD MOUNTFIELD ROAD

A 505
COOKSTOWN 36 2

Srule River

DERRY ROAD

MOUNTJOY ROAD

HOSPITAL

RUC Sta

KILLYCLOGHER ROAD

AGHNAMOYLE ROAD

BROOKMOUNT ROAD

School

BUS
Sta

P

Sch

Schools

CAMPSIE ROAD

School

HOSPITAL

School

Cannon River

School

Tourist Office
Tel. (028) 82247831

i

P

School

HOSPITAL ROAD

School

School

Drubragh River

TOWNVIEW AVE

DROMORE ROAD

CLANABOGAN ROAD

School

KEVLIN ROAD

DUBLIN ROAD

18

18

0 Km   ¼   ½   ¾   1
0 Mls   ¼   ½
Scale 1:23 000

HOSPITAL

School

HOSPITAL

A 32
DROMORE 11 7

A 5
BALLYGAWLEY 23 14

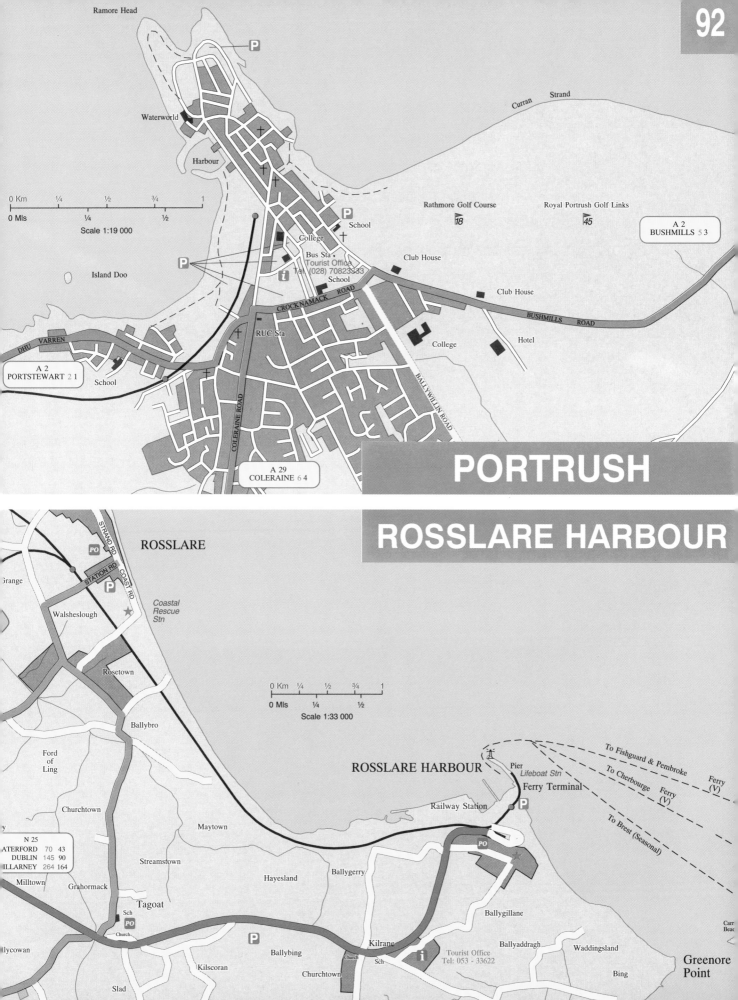

Ramore Head

P

Waterworld

Harbour

Curran   Strand

0 Km   ¼   ½   ¾   1

0 Mls   ¼   ½

Scale 1:19 000

Island Doo

Rathmore Golf Course

Royal Portrush Golf Links

18

45

A 2
BUSHMILLS 5 3

P

School

College

P

Bus Sta
Tourist Office
Tel (028) 70823333

i

School

Club House

CROCKNAMACK   ROAD

Club House

School

DHU VARREN

RUC Sta

College

Hotel

BUSHMILLS   ROAD

A 2
PORTSTEWART 2 1

School

COLERAINE ROAD

BALLYWILLIN ROAD

A 29
COLERAINE 6 4

PORTRUSH

ROSSLARE HARBOUR

ROSSLARE

PO

STRAND RD

STATION RD

COAST RD

Grange

P

Walsheslough

Coastal
Rescue
Stn

Rosetown

0 Km   ¼   ½   ¾   1

0 Mls   ¼   ½

Scale 1:33 000

Ballybro

Ford
of
Ling

To Fishguard & Pembroke

ROSSLARE HARBOUR

Pier

Ferry

Lifeboat Stn

To Cherbourge   Ferry
(V)

Churchtown

Maytown

Ferry Terminal

Railway Station

P

To Brest (Seasonal)

N 25
ATERFORD 70 43
DUBLIN 145 90
ILLARNEY 264 164

Streamstown

Hayesland

Ballygerry

PO

Milltown

Grahormack

Sch

Tagoat

PO

Church

P

Ballybing

Kilrane

Ballygillane

Ballyaddragh

Waddingsland

lycowan

Kilscoran

Church

Sch

Churchtown

i

Tourist Office
Tel: 053 - 33622

Greenore
Point

Slad

Carr
Beac

Bing

SLIGO

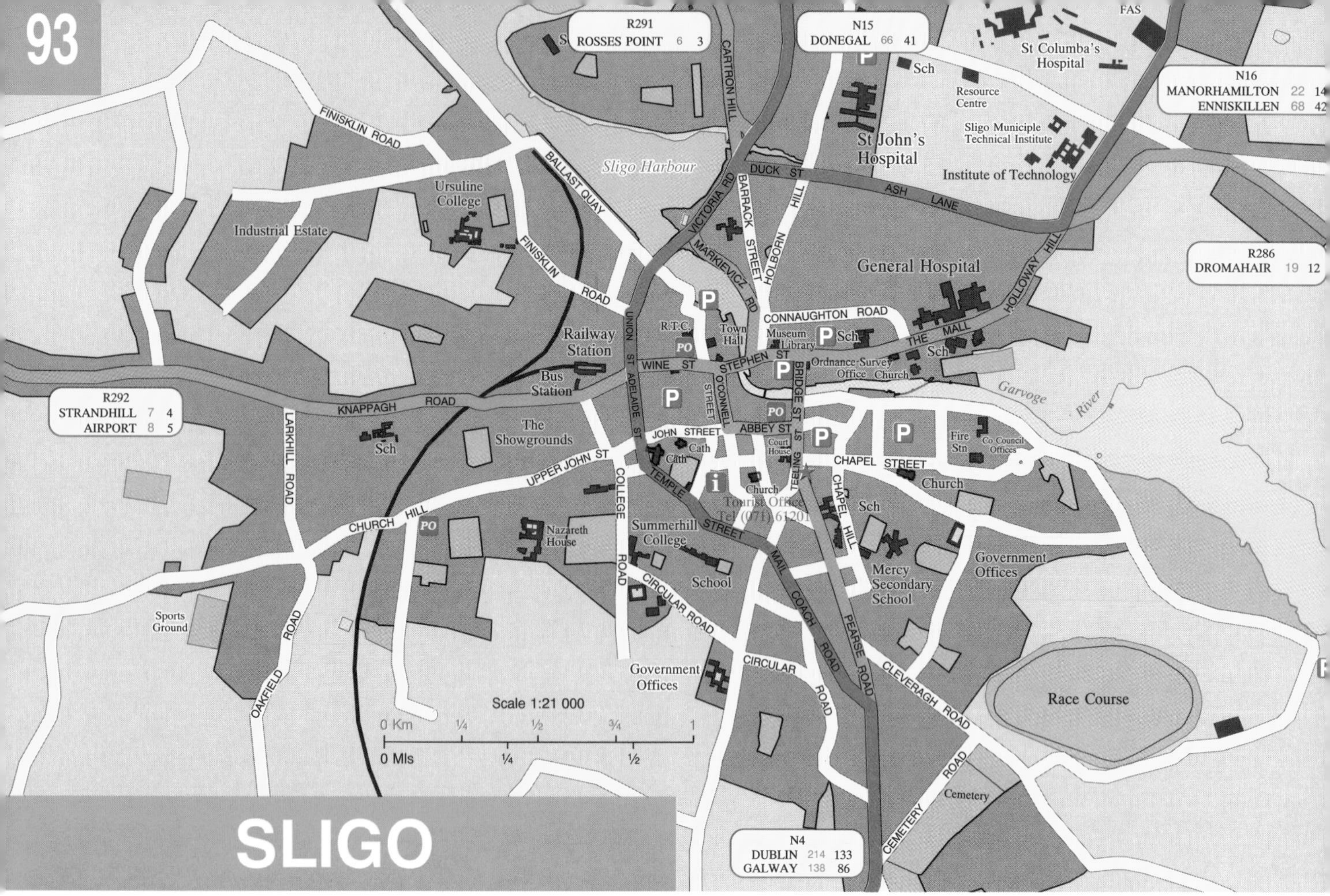
R291 ROSSES POINT 6 3
N15 DONEGAL 66 41
N16 MANORHAMILTON 22 14 ENNISKILLEN 68 42
R286 DROMAHAIR 19 12
R292 STRANDHILL 7 4 AIRPORT 8 5
N4 DUBLIN 214 133 GALWAY 138 86
FAS
St Columba's Hospital
Sch
Resource Centre
Sligo Municiple Technical Institute
St John's Hospital
Institute of Technology
Sligo Harbour
FINISKLIN ROAD
BALLAST QUAY
CARTRON HILL
DUCK ST
ASH LANE
Ursuline College
Industrial Estate
FINISKLIN ROAD
VICTORIA RD
BARRACK STREET
HOLBORN HILL
MARKIEVICZ RD
General Hospital
HOLLOWAY HILL
CONNAUGHTON ROAD
THE MALL
Railway Station
R.T.C.
Town Hall
Museum Library
Sch
Ordnance Survey Office
Church
Bus Station
UNION ST
WINE ST
STEPHEN ST
ADELAIDE ST
O'CONNELL STREET
BRIDGE ST
Garvoge River
KNAPPAGH ROAD
The Showgrounds
JOHN STREET
ABBEY ST
Court House
Cath
Fire Stn
Co Council Offices
Sch
LARKHILL ROAD
UPPER JOHN ST
TEMPLE STREET
Church
Tourist Office Tel (071) 61201
TEELING ST
CHAPEL STREET
Church
CHURCH HILL
COLLEGE ROAD
Nazareth House
Summerhill College
CHAPEL HILL
Sch
Government Offices
Mercy Secondary School
School
CIRCULAR ROAD
MAIL COACH ROAD
PEARSE ROAD
Sports Ground
OAKFIELD ROAD
Government Offices
CIRCULAR ROAD
CLEVERAGH ROAD
Race Course
Scale 1:21 000
0 Km ¼ ½ ¾ 1
0 Mls ¼ ½
CEMETERY ROAD
Cemetery

TRALEE

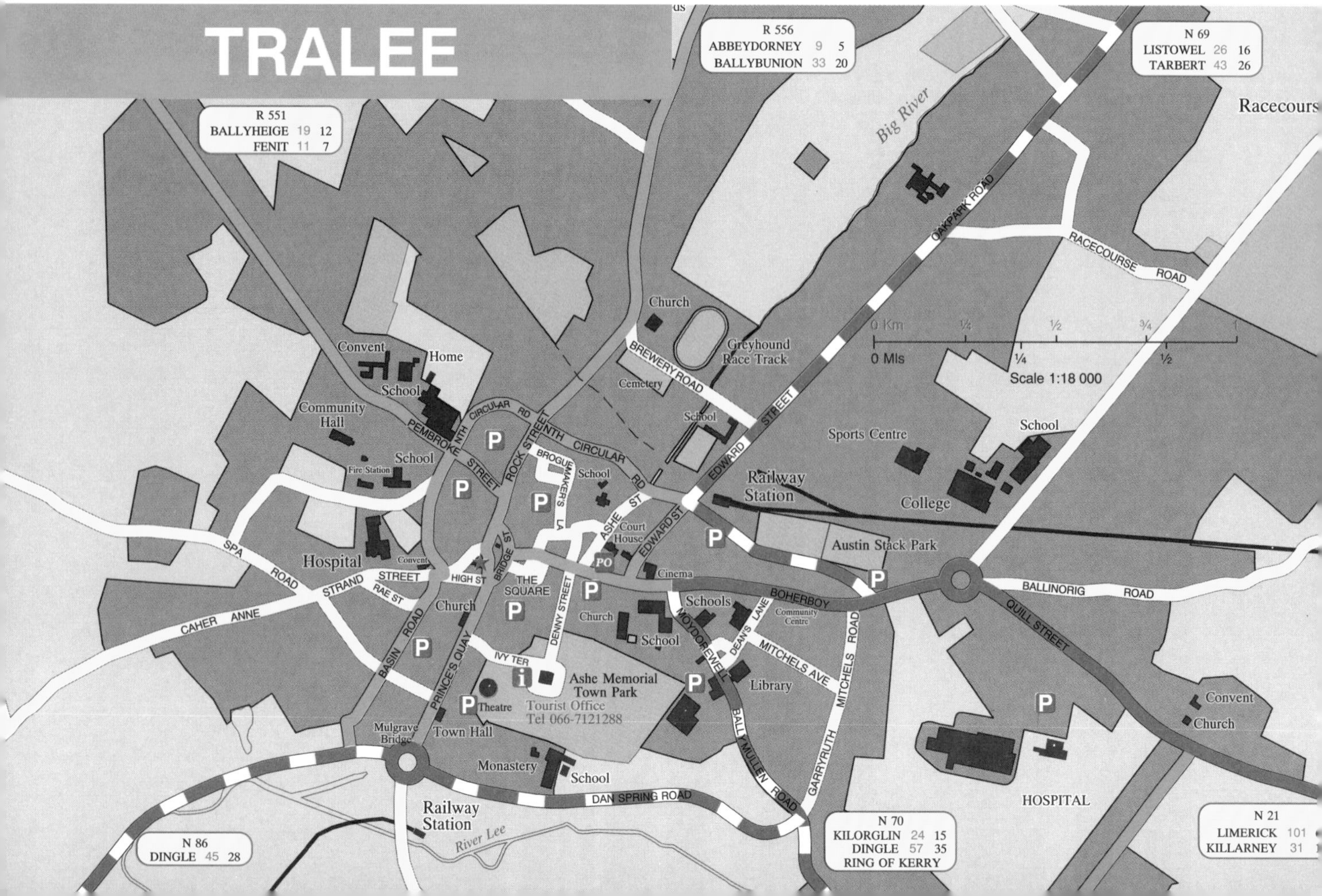
R 556 ABBEYDORNEY 9 5 BALLYBUNION 33 20
N 69 LISTOWEL 26 16 TARBERT 43 26
Racecourse
R 551 BALLYHEIGE 19 12 FENIT 11 7
Big River
OAKPARK ROAD
RACECOURSE ROAD
Church
Greyhound Race Track
0 Km ¼ ½ ¾ 1
0 Mls ¼ ½
Scale 1:18 000
Convent
Home
School
BREWERY ROAD
Cemetery
Community Hall
CIRCULAR RD
School
EDWARD STREET
Sports Centre
School
PEMBROKE STREET
NTH CIRCULAR RD
ROCK STREET
BROGUE MAKER'S LA
School
Fire Station
School
Railway Station
College
ASHE ST
Court House
EDWARD ST
Austin Stack Park
SPA ROAD
Hospital
Convent
HIGH ST
BRIDGE ST
Cinema
BOHERBOY
BALLINORIG ROAD
STRAND STREET
RAE ST
THE SQUARE
Schools
QUILL STREET
CAHER ANNE
Church
DENNY STREET
Church
DEAN'S LANE
Community Centre
BASIN ROAD
MOYDERWELL
School
MITCHELS AVE
MITCHELS ROAD
IVY TER
Ashe Memorial Town Park
Library
Convent
Church
PRINCE'S QUAY
Theatre
Tourist Office Tel 066-7121288
Mulgrave Bridge
Town Hall
BALLYMULLEN ROAD
GARRYRUTH
Monastery
School
HOSPITAL
DAN SPRING ROAD
Railway Station
River Lee
N 86 DINGLE 45 28
N 70 KILORGLIN 24 15 DINGLE 57 35 RING OF KERRY
N 21 LIMERICK 101 KILLARNEY 31

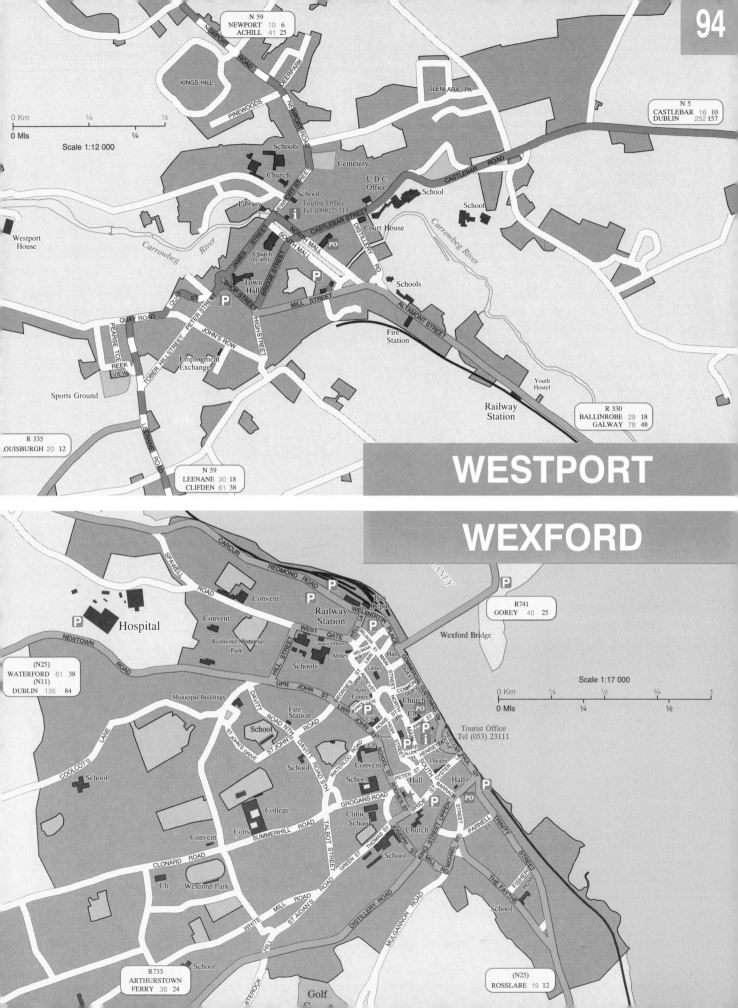

WESTPORT

WEXFORD

Westport map labels:

N 59
NEWPORT 10 6
ACHILL 41 25

N 5
CASTLEBAR 16 10
DUBLIN 252 157

Scale 1:12 000

0 Km ¼ ½
0 Mls ¼

KINGS HILL

GLENLARA PK

PINEWOODS

DEERPARK

NEWPORT ROAD

Schools

Cemetery

Church

CASTLEBAR ROAD

U.D.C. Office

School

School

School

Carrowbeg River

Library

Westport House

Carrowbeg River

School

Tourist Office
Tel (098)25711

CASTLEBAR STREET

Court House

NORTH MALL

PO

DISTILLERY RD

JAMES STREET

SOUTH MALL

Church (Cath)

Schools

QUAY ST

SHOP STREET

Town Hall

BRIDGE STREET

MILL STREET

ALTAMONT STREET

QUAY ROAD

PEARSE TCE

TOBER HILL STREET

PETER STREET

JOHN'S ROW

HIGH STREET

Fire Station

REEK VIEW

Employment Exchange

Youth Hostel

LEENANE ROAD

Sports Ground

Railway Station

R 335
LOUISBURGH 20 12

N 59
LEENANE 30 18
CLIFDEN 61 38

R 330
BALLINROBE 29 18
GALWAY 78 48

Wexford map labels:

CARCUR

SPAWELL ROAD

REDMOND ROAD

P

Convent

P

Railway Station

SLANEY

P

R741
GOREY 40 25

P

Hospital

Convent

Redmond Memorial Park

WEST GATE

Council Offices

WELLINGTON PLACE

Bus Depot

Wexford Bridge

NEWTOWN ROAD

HILL STREET

Schools

Abbey

Hall

COMMERCIAL QUAY

Scale 1:17 000

0 Km ¼ ½ ¾ 1
0 Mls ¼ ½

(N25)
WATERFORD 61 38
(N11)
DUBLIN 135 84

UPR JOHN ST

SELSKAR ST

Library

GEORGE ST

ABBEY ST LWR

COMMON QUAY

Church Ch

PO

Municipal Buildings

COOLCOT'S LANE

DAVITT ROAD NTH

Fire Station

School

ST JOHN'S DRIVE

DAVITT ROAD STH

LWR JOHN ST

Arts Centre

ROWE HIGH ST

Ch

ANNE ST

NORTH MAIN ST

CRESCENT QUAY

PAUL QY

Tourist Office
Tel (053) 23111

i

School

WATERLOO ROAD

Theatre

SCHOOL ST

P

Allen ST

HENRIETTA ST

Convent

School

Peter ST

Hall

SOUTH MAIN ST

OYSTER

Theatre

Hall

College

GROGANS ROAD

Clinic

School

BRIDE ST

ROCHE'S ST

Church

BARRACK ST

PO

P

Convent

SUMMERHILL ROAD

TALBOT STREET

GREEN ST

JOSEPH ST

THOMAS ST

School

KING ST

MILL RD

MICHAEL ST

PARNELL ST

TRINITY STREET

FISHERS ROW

Convent

CLONARD ROAD

Ch

Wexford Park

WHITE MILL ROAD

ST AIDAN'S ROAD

DISTILLERY ROAD

MULGANNON ROAD

THE FAYTHE

School

R733
ARTHURSTOWN FERRY 38 24

School

(N25)
ROSSLARE 19 12

Golf

TOURIST OFFICES

REPUBLIC OF IRELAND

The Tourist Offices listed below operate throughout the year, except for those marked thus (*) which are open during the summer months. A full list is availabe from any Bord Fáilte - Irish Tourist Board Office.

Adare	061 396255	***Glendalough**	0404 45688
Aran Islands (Kilronan)	099 61263	***Gorey**, Town Centre	055 21248
*Arklow	0402 32484	***Kildare**	045 522696
*Athlone	0902 94630	**Kilkenny**, Rose Inn Street	056 51500
Baggot St. Bridge(Head Office)	01 602 4000	**Killarney**, Town Hall	064 31633
Blarney	021 381624	***Kinsale**	021 772234
Brú na Bóinne Visitor Centre (Newgrange)	041 9880305	***Knock Airport**	094 67247
Bundoran	072 41350	**Letterkenny**, Derry Road	074 21160
*Cahir	052 41453	**Limerick City**, Arthur's Quay	061 317522
Carlow, College Street	0503 31554	***Longford**	043 46566
*Carrick-on-Shannon	078 20170	***New Ross**	051 421857
*Cashel (Town Hall)	062 61333	***Monaghan**, Market House	047 81122
*Cavan, Farnham Street	049 31942	**Mullingar**, Dublin Road	044 48650
*Cliffs of Moher, Liscannor	065 7081171	**Portlaoise**	0502 21178
*Clonmacnoise	0905 74134	***Rosslare**, Kilrane	053 33622
*Clonmel	052 22960	**Shannon Airport**	061 471664
Cork City, Tourist House, Grand Parade	021 273251	**Skibbereen**, Town Hall	028 21766
*Dingle	066 51188	**Sligo**, Temple Street	071 61201
*Donegal Town, The Quay	073 21148	***Tipperary**	062 51457
*Drogheda	041 9837070	***Tramore**	051 281572
Dublin, Suffolk Street, Dublin 2.	01 6057700	**Tralee**, Ashe Memorial Hall	066 7121288
	1850 230330	**Trim**	046 37111
Dundalk, Market Square	042 9335484	***Tullamore**	0506 52617
Dungarvan	058 41741	**Waterford**, 41 The Quay	051 875823
*Dunglow	075 21297	**Waterford Crystal** Visitor Centre	051 358397
Ennis, Clare Road	065 6828366	**Westport**, The Mall	098 25711
*Enniscorthy(The Castle)	054 34699	**Wexford**, Crescent Quay	053 23111
Galway, Victoria Place, Eyre Square	091 563081	**Wicklow**, Fitzwilliam Square	0404 69117

INTERNATIONAL OFFICES

BELFAST, 53Castle Street	048 327888
DERRY, 8 Bishop Street	01504 369501
LONDON, 150 New Bond Street	0171 493 3201
LONDON, 12 Regent Street	0171 839 8416
PARIS, 33 Rue de Miromesnil	0153 43 1212
MADRID,Claudio Coello 73	91 577 1787
MILAN, via S Maria Segreta 6	02 869 0541
FRANKFURT, Untermainanlage 7	069 236492
AMSTERDAM, Spuistraat 106-108	020 622 3101
BRUSSELS, Avenue de Beaulieu 25	02 673 9940
STOCKHOLM, Sipyllegatan 49	08 662 8510
COPENHAGAN, Klostergarden, Amagertory 293	33 15 8045
NEW YORK, 345 Park Avenue	212 418 0800
SYDNEY, 36 Carrington Street	02 9299 6177
TOKYO, 2-10-7 Kojimachi, Chiyoda-ku	03 5275 1611

NORTHERN IRELAND TOURIST BOARD

www.discovernorthernireland.com - Email:info@nitb.com

HEAD OFFICE		(028) 9023 1221
59 North Street, Belfast. BT1 1NB	Fax	(028) 9024 0960
DUBLIN		01 679 1977
16 Nassau Street, Dublin 2.	Fax	01 679 1863
	Call Save	1850 230 230
LONDON		0171 355 5040
11 Berkley Street, London. W1X 5AD	Fax	0171 409 0487
GLASGOW		0141 204 4454
135 Buchanon Street, Glasgow. G1 2JA	Fax	0141 204 4033
U.S.A.		212 922 0101
551 Fifth Avenue, Suite 701, New York NY 10176	Fax	212 922 0099
CANADA		416 925 6368
111 Avenue Road, Suite 450, Toronto. M5R 3J8	Fax	416 961 2175
FRANCE		139 21 9380
3 Rue de Pontoise, 78100 St, Germain-en-Laye	Fax	139 21 9390
GERMANY		069 23 4504
Taunusstrasse 52-60, 60329 Frankfurt/Main.	Fax	069 23 3480
AUSTRALIA		(02) 92996177
36 Carrington Street, Sydney, NSW 2000	Fax	(02) 9299 6323
NEW ZEALAND		(09) 379 3708
87 Queen Street, Private Bag 92136,Auckland 1, DX 69051	Fax	(09) 309 0725

NETWORKED TOURIST INFORMATION CENTRES

The Tourist Information Centre Network provides a first-class information service for visitors to Northern Ireland and for local residents. Services available at these offices include : free information on the local area - tourist attractions, accommodations, where to eat, events; free information on holidays throughout Northern Ireland; accommodation booking for Ireland and the U.K.

Belfast, Belfast Welcome Centre, 35 Donegal Place	(028) 9024 6609
Antrim, 16 High Street	(028) 9442 8331
Armagh. Old Bank Building, 40 English Street	(028) 3752 1800
Ballycastle, Sheskburn House, 7 Mary Street	(028) 2076 2024
Ballymena, 76 Chruch Street	(028) 2563 8494
Banbridge, Gateway Tourist Information Centre, Newry Road	(028) 4062 3322
Bangor, 34 Quay Street	(028) 9127 0069
Carrickfergus, Knight Ride, Antrim Street	(028) 9336 6455
Coleraine, Railway Road	(028) 7034 4723
Cookstown, The Burnavon, Burn Road	(028) 8676 6727
Downpatrick, The St. Patrick Centre Market Street	(028) 4461 2233
Enniskillen, Fermanagh Tourist Information Centre, Wellington Road	(028) 6632 3110
Giant's Causeway, 44 Causeway Road, Bushmills	(028) 2073 1855
Hillsborough, The Courthouse, The Square	(028) 9268 9717
Kilkeel, 6 Newcastle Street	(028) 4176 2525
Killymaddy, 190 Ballygawley Road, Dungannon	(028) 8776 7259
Larne, Narrow Gauge Road	(028) 2826 0088
Limavady, Council Offices, 7 Connell Street	(028) 7776 0307
Lisburn, Irish Linen Centre & Lisburn Museum, Market Square	(028) 9266 0038
Londonderry, 44 Foyle Street	(028) 7126 7284
Newcastle, 10-14 Central Promenade	(028) 4372 2222
Newtownards, 31 Regent Street	(028) 9182 6846
Omagh, 1 Market Street	(028) 8224 7831
Portaferry, The Stables, Castle Street	(028) 4272 9882
Portrush, Dunluce Centre, Sandhill Drive	(028) 7082 3333
Strabane, Abercorn Square	(028) 7188 3735

Affiliated to the Golf Union of Ireland
This listing is by Province and County
The name of the Golf Club is preceded by the number of holes and followed
by a page number and a reference for the grid square in which the golf location symbol appears.

CONNAUGHT

Co.GALWAY
18	Ardacong	32 E1
18	Athenry	32 E4
18	Ballinasloe	33 A4
18	Bearna	31 C4
27	Connemara	29 B2
9	Connemara Isles	30 F3
18	Curra West	32 G5
18	Galway	31 C4
18	Galway Bay	31 D4
9	Glenlo Abbey	31 C4
18	Gort	42 E1
18	Loughrea	32 G5
9	Mountbellew	32 G2
18	Oughterard	30 H2
18	Portumna	43 A1
18	Tuam	32 E2

Co LEITRIM
9	Ballinamore	17 A5
9	Carrick-on-Shannon	25 A1

Co MAYO
9	Achill	21 C1
18	Ballina	14 H5
18	Ballinrobe	22 H5
9	Ballyhaunis	24 E3
18	Belmullet	13 B3
18	Castlebar	22 H3
18	Claremorris	23 D4
9	Mulranny	22 E2
9	Swinford	23 D2
18	Westport	22 F3

Co ROSCOMMON
18	Athlone	33 C2
9	Ballaghaderreen	24 G2
9	Boyle	25 A1
9	Castlerea	24 G3
18	Roscommon	25 A5
9	Strokestown	25 B4

Co SLIGO
9	Ballymote	15 D5
27	Co Sligo	15 D2
18	Enniscrone	14 H4
18	Strandhill	15 D3
9	Tubbercurry	15 C5

LEINSTER

Co CARLOW
9	Borris	53 B2
18	Carlow	45 B4
18	Mount Wolseley	45 C4

Co DUBLIN
18	Balbriggan	28 G5
18	Balcarrick	36 G2
18	Ballinascorney	36 E4
18	Beaverstown	36 G1
18	Beech Park	35 D4
18	City West	36 E4
18	Christy O'Connor	36 E4
18	Coldwinters	36 F2
18	Corballis	36 G2
27	Corrstown	36 F2
27	Donabate	36 G2
18	Dublin Mountain	36 E4
18	Dun Laoire	36 G4
9	Finnstown	36 E3
18	Forrest Little	36 F2
18	Glencullen	36 F2
18	Hermitage	36 F2
18	Hollywood Lakes	36 F1
18	Island	36 G2
9	Killiney	36 G4
18	Kilternan	36 G4
18	Lucan	36 E3
18	Luttrellstown	36 E3
27	Malahide	36 G2
18	Old Conna	36 G4
27	Portmarnock	36 G2
9	Rush	36 G1
18	St Margarets	36 F2
18	Skerries	36 G1
18	Slade Valley	36 E4
18	Swords	36 F2
18	Turvey	36 G1
18	Westmanstown	36 E3
18	Woodbrook	36 G4

DUBLIN CITY
9	Carrickmines	36 G4
18	Castle	36 F4
18	Clontarf	36 F3
36	Deer Park	36 G3
18	Edmondstown	36 F4
18	Elmgreen	36 E3
18	Elm Park	36 F4
9	Foxrock	36 G4
24	Grange	36 F4
27	Hollystown	36 E2
9	Hazel Grove	36 E4
18	Howth	36 G3
9	Kilmashogue	36 F4
18	Milltown	36 F4
18	Newlands	36 E4
9	Rathfarnham	36 F4
18	Royal Dublin	36 G3
18	St. Anne's	36 G3
18	Stackstown	36 F4
9	Sutton	36 G3

Co LAOIS
9	Abbeyleix	44 G3
18	Heath	44 H1
18	Mountrath	44 F2
18	Portarlington	34 H5
18	Rathdowney	44 E4

Co KILDARE
18	Athy	45 B2
36	Bodenstown	35 C4
18	Castlewarden	35 D4
9	Celbridge	35 D3
9	Cill Dara	35 B5
9	Clongowes	35 C3
18	Craddockstown	35 D5
18	Curragh	35 B5
18	Highfield	35 A3
18	Kilkea Castle	35 D4
18	Killeen	35 D4
18	Knockanally	35 C3
18	K Club	35 D4
9	Leixlip	36 E3
18	Naas	35 D4
18	Newbridge	35 D4
18	Woodlands	35 B4

Co KILKENNY
18	Callan	52 G2
9	Castlecomer	44 H4
18	Kilkenny	52 H1
18	Mount Juliet	52 H2
9	Mountain View	52 H3
18	Waterford	53 A5

Co LONGFORD
18	Co Longford	25 D4

Co LOUTH
18	Ardee	27 D2
18	Co Louth	28 F4
18	Dundalk	28 E1
18	Greenore	19 D5
18	Killinbeg	28 E1
9	Townley Hall	28 E4
18	Seapoint	28 F3

Co MEATH
18	Ashbourne	36 E1
27	Black Bush	35 D1
9	Gormanstown College	28 F5
36	Headfort	27 B4
18	Kilcock	35 C2
18	Laytown & Bettystown	28 F4
18	Moor Park	27 D5
18	Navan	27 C4
27	Royal Tara	27 C5
9	South Meath	27 A5
9	Summerhill	35 C2
18	Trim	35 B1

Co OFFALY
18	Birr	43 C1
18	Castle Barna	34 G4
18	Edenderry	35 A3
18	Esker Hills	34 E4
18	Moate	33 D3
18	Mount Temple	33 D2
18	Mullingar	34 G2
18	Tullamore	34 F4

Co WESTMEATH
9	Ballinlough Castle	27 A5
18	Delvin Castle	26 H5
18	Glasson	33 C2

Co WEXFORD
18	Courtown	54 F1
18	Enniscorthy	53 D3
18	New Ross	53 A4
30	Rosslare	54 E5
18	St.Helen's Bay	54 F5
9	Tara Glen	46 G5
18	Wexford	54 E4

Co WICKLOW
18	Arklow	46 G4
9	Baltinglass	45 C3
18	Blainroe	46 H2
9	Boystown	35 D5
9	Bray	36 G5
18	Charlesland	36 H5
18	Coollattin	46 E5
18	Delgany	36 G5
9	Djouce Mountain	46 G1
18	Druid's Glen	46 G1
18	European	46 H3
18	Glen of the Downs	36 G5
18	Glenmalure	46 F3
18	Greystones	36 G5
9	Kilcoole	46 H1
18	Powerscourt	36 G5
18	Rathsallagh	45 C2
18	Roundwood	46 G1
18	Tulfarris	45 D1
9	Vartry Lakes	46 F1
18	Wicklow	46 H2
18	Woodenbridge	46 F4

MUNSTER

Co CLARE
9	Clonlara	42 G5
18	Dromoland	41 D4
9	East Clare	42 F3
18	Ennis	41 D4
9	Kilkee	39 D5
18	Kilrush	49 A1
36	Lahinch	40 F3
18	Shannon	41 D5
9	Spanish Point	40 F4
18	Woodstock	41 D4

Co CORK

18 Bandon	68 E1
18 Bantry Bay	66 H1
9 Berehaven	66 F2
27 Charleville	50 F4
9 Cobh	61 A5
9 Coosheen	66 H3
18 Cork	60 H4
9 Doneraile	60 F1
18 Douglas	60 H5
9 Dunmore	67 D3
18 East Cork	61 A4
18 Fermoy	60 H2
18 Fernhill	60 H5
18 Fota Island	60 H4
9 Frankfield	60 G5
9 Glengarriff	66 H1
18 Harbour Point	60 H4
18 Kanturk	59 D1
27 Kinsale	68 G1
18 Lee Valley	60 F4
18 Macroom	59 D4
18 Mahon	60 H4
18 Mallow	60 F2
15 Mitchelstown	50 H5
18 Monkstown	60 H5
18 Muskerry	60 F4
9 Raffeen Creek	60 H5
18 Skibbereen	67 B3
18 Youghal	61 D4

Co KERRY

9 Ardfert	48 G4
9 Ballybeggan Park	48 G5
36 Ballybunion	48 G2
9 Ballyheigue Castle	48 F4
18 Beaufort	58 G2
9 Castlegregory	48 E5
18 Ceann Sibeal	57 B1
18 Dooks	58 E2
18 Kenmare	58 H4
9 Kerries	48 G5
54 Killarney	58 H2
18 Killorglin	58 G2
9 Listowel	49 A3
12 Parknasilla	58 F5
18 Ring of Kerry	58 G4
9 Ross	58 H3
18 Tralee	48 F5
18 Waterville	57 C5

Co LIMERICK

9 Abbeyfeale	49 B4
18 Adare Manor	50 E2
18 Castletroy	50 G1
18 Limerick	50 F1
18 Limerick Co	50 G1
18 Newcastle West	49 C3
18 Rathbane	50 F1

Co TIPPERARY

18 Ballykisteen	51 A3
18 Cahir Park	51 C4
18 Clonmel	52 E4
18 Co Tipperary	51 B2
18 Nenagh	43 B3
9 Rockwell	51 C3
18 Roscrea	43 D3
18 Slievenamon	51 D3
9 Templemore	43 D5
18 Thurles	51 D1
18 Tipperary	51 A3

Co WATERFORD

18 Carrick-on-Suir	52 F4
18 Dungarvan	62 E2
18 Dunmore East	63 B3
18 Faithlegg	53 A5
18 Gold Coast	62 F2
9 Lismore	61 C2
18 Tramore	62 H1
18 Waterford Castle	53 A5
18 West Waterford	62 E2

ULSTER

Co ANTRIM

18 Antrim	11 C3
18 Ballycastle	5 D2
18 Ballyclare	11 D2
18 Ballymena	11 C1
9 Burnfield House	12 E3
9 Bushfoot	4 G2
18 Cairndhu	12 E1
18 Carrickfergus	12 F3
9 Cushendall	6 E4
18 Glangorm Castle	11 B1
18 Gracehill	4 H3
18 Greenacres	11 D3
9 Greenisland	12 E3
18 Hilton Templepatrick	11 D3
18 Lambeg	11 D5
18 Larne	12 F1
18 Lisburn	11 D5
18 Loughgall	19 A1
9 Mallusk	11 D3
18 Massereene	11 C3
18 Rathmore	4 F2
45 Royal Portrush	4 F2
18 Whitehead	12 F2

Co ARMAGH

18 Ashfield	19 A5
9 Cloverhill	19 A5
18 Co Armagh	18 H2
18 Edenmore	19 C1
18 Lurgan	19 B1
18 Portadown	19 B1
18 Silverwood	19 B1
18 Tandragee	19 B2

BELFAST

18 Balmoral	12 E4
18 Belvoir Park	12 E5
9 Cliftonville	12 E4
18 Dunmurry	12 E5
18 Fortwilliam	12 E4
9 Gilnahirk	12 F4
18 Knock	12 F4
27 Malone	12 E5
18 Mount Ober	12 E5
9 Ormeau	12 E4
18 Shandon Park	12 E4

Co CAVAN

9 Belturbet	17 C5
9 Blacklion	16 H3
9 Cabra Castle	27 B2
18 Co Cavan	26 G1
18 Slieve Russell	17 B4
9 Virginia	27 A3

Co DONEGAL

18 Ballybofey & Stranorlar	9 A2
36 Ballyliffin	3 A2
9 Buncrana	3 A3
18 Bundoran	8 F5
9 Chloic Cheann Fhaola	2 E3
9 Cruit Island	1 C5
18 Donegal	8 G4
18 Dunfanaghy	2 F3
9 Gaoth Dobhair	1 D4
18 Greencastle	3 D2
18 Letterkenny	2 H5
18 Narin & Portnoo	8 E2
18 North West	3 A4
9 Otway	3 A3
18 Portsalon	2 H3
9 Redcastle	3 C3
26 Rosapenna	2 G3

Co DOWN

18 Ardglass	20 G3
9 Ardminnan	20 H1
18 Banbridge	19 C2
18 Bangor	12 G3
36 Blackwood	12 F4
18 Bright Castle	20 F3
18 Carnalea	12 F3
36 Clandeboye	12 F4
9 Crossgar	20 F1
18 Donaghadee	12 G3
18 Downpatrick	20 G2
18 Down Royal	11 D5
9 Helen's Bay	12 F3
18 Holywood	12 F4
18 Kilkeel	19 D5
18 Kirkistown Castle	20 H1
9 Mahee Island	12 G5
18 Mourne	20 E3
18 Ringdufferin	20 G1

18 Rockmount	12 E5
18 Royal Belfast	12 F4
36 Royal Co Down	20 E3
18 Scrabo Newtownards	12 F4
18 Spa	20 E1
9 Temple	20 E1
18 Warrenpoint	19 C5

Co FERMANAGH

18 Castle Hume	17 B2
18 Enniskillen	17 B2

Co LONDONDERRY

9 Brown Trout	4 H4
27 Castlerock	4 E3
27 City of Derry	3 B5
27 Foyle	3 B4
9 Kilrea	4 G5
9 Manor	4 G5
18 Moyola Park	11 A2
45 Portstewart	4 E3
18 Roe Park	3 D4
9 Traad Ponds	11 A3

Co MONAGHAN

9 Castleblaney	18 H5
9 Clones	17 D4
18 Mannan Castle	27 C1
18 Nuremore	27 C1
18 Rossmore	18 F3

Co TYRONE

9 Aughnacloy	18 F1
9 Benburb Valley	18 H1
18 Dungannon	10 G5
9 Fintona	9 D5
18 Killymoon	
18 Cookstown	10 H4
18 Newtownstewart	9 C3
18 Omagh	9 D4
18 Strabane	9 C2

GAZETTEER

This Gazetteer lists cities, town and villages in alphabetical order. The figure in bold type immediately following the name is the number of the page on which the place appears and the alphanumeric reference indicates the appropriate grid square.

Example:- Allenwood / Fiodh Alúine   **35** B4

Allenwood will be found on page **35** square B4

A

Abbey / An Mhainistir	**42** H1
Abbeydorney / Mainistir Ó dTorna	**48** G4
Abbeyfeale / Mainistir na Feile	**49** B4
Abbeylara / Mainistir Leatghratha	**26** F4
Abbeyleix / Mainistir Laoise	**44** G3
Abbeyshrule / Mainistir Shruthla	**34** E1
Abington	**50** H1
Achill Sound / Gob an Choire	**21** D1
Achonry / Achadh Conaire	**15** C5
Aclare / Áth An Chláir	**24** E1
Adamstown / Maigh Arnai	**53** C4
Adare / Áth Dara	**50** E2
Addergoole Co Mayo	**23** D3
Addergoole Co Galway	**31** D3
Adrigole	**66** G1
Aghaboe / Achadh Bhó	**44** F3
Aghaboy	**25** D3
Aghabullogue / Achadh Bolg	**60** E4
Aghacashel	**16** H5
Aghada	**61** A5
Aghadiffin	**24** F2
Aghadoon	**13** B3
Aghadowey / Achadh Dubhtaigh	**4** F4
Aghadown	**67** A3
Aghagallon / Achadh Gallan	**11** C5
Aghagower / Achadh Ghobhair	**22** G4
Aghalee / Achadh Lí	**11** C5
Aghamore / Achadh Mór	**25** C2
Co Leitrim / Liatroim	
Aghamore / Achadh Mór	**24** E3
Co Mayo / Maigh Eo	
Aghavas / Achadh an Mheasa	**25** D1
Aghern	**61** A2
Aghleam	**13** B4
Aghnacliff / Achadh na Cloiche	**26** E3
Aghnamullen / Achadh na Muileann	**18** F5
Agivey	**4** F4
Aglish / An Eaglais	**57** D2
Co Kerry / Ciarraí	
Aglish / An Eaglais	**43** B2
Co Tipperary / Tiobraid Árann	
Aglish / An Eaglais	**61** D2
Co Waterford / Port Láirge	
Ahafona	**48** G2
Ahakista	**66** G3
Ahascragh / Ath Eascrach	**32** H3
Aherla / An Eatharla	**60** F5
Ahoghill / Achadh Eochaille	**11** B1
Ailladie	**40** F1
Aldergrove / An Garrán Fearnóige	**11** C4
Allen	**35** B4
Allenwood / Fiodh Alúine	**35** B4
Allihies / Na hAitichi	**65** D2
Allistragh / An tAilastrach	**18** H2
Alloon Lower	**32** G3
Altnapaste	**8** H2
An Greata Mór	**13** B3
Anascaul / Abhainn an Scáil	**57** D1
Anglesborough	**51** A4
Anlore	**18** E4
Annacarriga	**42** G4
Annacarty / Áth na Cairte	**51** B2
Annaclone / Eanach Cluana	**19** C2
Annacloy / Áth na Cloiche	**20** F2
Annacotty	**50** G1
Annacurragh	**46** E4
Annagap	**57** D1
Annagary / Anagaire	**1** C5
Annagassan / Áth na gCasán	**28** E2
Annagh Co Limerick	**50** G1
Annagh Co Roscommon	**24** G4
Annagh Neal	**42** F3
Annaghdown	**31** C3
Annaghmore / Eanach Mór	**25** C5
Annahilt / Eanach Eiulte	**20** E1
Annalong / Áth na Long	**20** E5
Annamoe	**46** F2
Annascaul / Abhainn an Scáil	**57** D1
Annaville	**43** C2
Annayalla / Eanaigh Gheala	**18** G4
Annestown / Bun Abha	**62** G2
Annfield	**43** C5
Annsborough / Baiuule Anna	**20** E3
Antrim / Aontroim	**11** C3
Araglin / Airglinn	**61** B1
Archerstown / Baile an Airsirigh	**26** H5
Ardagh / Ardach	**49** C3
Co Limerick / Luimneach	
Ardagh / Ardach	**26** E5
Co Longdord / An Longfort	
Ardagh / Ardach	**27** C2
Co Meath / An Mhí	
Ardnagunna	**61** D1
Ardan	**34** F4
Ardanew	**35** B2
Ardara / Ard an Rátha	**8** E2
Ardattin / Ard Aitinn	**45** C5
Ardbane	**8** F3
Ardcath	**28** E5
Ardconnell	**48** F4
Ardcrony / Ard Cróine	**43** A3
Ardee / Baile Átha Fhirdhia	**27** D2
Ardfert / Ard Fhearta	**48** F4
Ardfeld / Ard ó bhFicheallaigh	**67** D3
Ardfinnan / Ard Fhionáin	**51** C5
Ardglass / Ard Ghlais	**20** G3
Co Down / An Dún	
Ardgroom / Dhá Dhrom	**66** E1
Ardkearagh	**57** D5
Ardkeen / Ard Caoin	**20** H1
Ardkill	**23** C5
Ardlea	**44** G2
Ardlougher / Ard Luachra	**17** B5
Ardmore / Aird Mhór	**61** D4
Ardmorney	**34** F3
Ardnacrusha	**42** F5
Ardnasodan	**32** E3
Ardpatrick / Ard Pádraig	**50** G4
Ardra	**61** A5
Ardrah Co Cork	**67** A1
Ardrahan / Ard Raithin	**32** E5
Ardress	**19** A1
Ardrigole	**66** G1
Ardscull	**45** B2
Ardstraw / Ard Sratha	**9** C3
Ardtrea / Ard Tré	**10** H4
Arigna / An Airgnigh	**16** G5
Arklow / An tInbhear Mór	**46** G4
Arless	**45** A3
Armagh / Ard Mhacha	**18** H2
Armoy / Oirthear Maí	**4** H3
Arney	**17** B3
Arranagh	**49** C4
Arthurstown / Colmán	**53** B5
Articlave / Ard an Chléibh	**4** E3
Artigarvan / Ard Tí Garbháin	**9** C1
Arvagh	**26** E2
Ashbourne / Cill Dhéagláin	**36** E1
Ashford / Áth na Fuinseoige	**46** G2
Ashhill	**51** D2
Askamore / An Easca Mhór	**54** E1
Askanagap	**46** E3
Askeaton / Eas Géitine	**49** D1
Astee / Eas Daoi	**48** H2
Athavallie	**23** C3
Athboy / Baile Átha Buí	**27** B5
Athea / Áth an tSléibhe	**49** B3
Athenry / Baile Átha an Rí	**32** F4
Athgarvan / Áth Garbháin	**35** C5
Athlacca / An tÁth Lacach	**50** F3
Athleague / Áth Liag	**33** A1
Athlone / Baile Átha Luain	**33** C2
Athnid	**43** D5
Athy / Baile Átha Í	**45** A2
Attanagh / Áth Tanaí	**44** G4
Attical / Áth Tí Chathail	**19** D5
Atticoffey	**33** A4
Attiregan	**32** H3
Attymass / Áth Tí an Mheasaigh	**14** H5
Attymon / Áth Tiomáin	**32** F3
Auburn	**33** D1
Aucloggeen	**31** D3
Aughacasla	**48** E5
Augher / Eochair	**18** E1
Aughfad	**53** D5
Aughils	**58** F1
Aughinish / Eachinis	**31** C5
Aughnacloy / Achadh na Cloiche	**18** F1
Aughnacleagh	**11** A1
Aughrim Co Clare	**41** D2
Aughrim / Eachroim	**32** H4
Co Galway / Gaillimh	
Aughrim / Eachroim	**46** F3
Co Wicklow / Cill Mhantáin	
Avoca / Abhóca	**46** G3

B

Name	Grid
Baconstown	35 C2
Bagenalstown / Muine Bheag	45 B5
Baileysmill / Muileann Bhaile	20 E1
Bailieborough / Colillan Chollaigh	27 A2
Balbriggan / Baile Brigin	28 G5
Balla / Balla	23 C3
Ballaba	42 E1
Ballady	68 G1
Ballagh / An Bealach Co Limerick / Luimneach	49 C4
Ballagh Co. Roscommon	33 B1
Ballagh Co Roscommon	25 B4
Ballagh Co Tipperary	51 C2
Ballagh Co Wexford	53 C4
Ballaghaderreen / Bealach An Doirín	24 G2
Ballaghbehy	49 B4
Ballaghboy	51 D2
Ballaghkeen / An Bealach	54 E3
Ballaghmore	44 E3
Ballard	34 F4
Ballardiggan	42 F1
Ballare	64 G3
Balleen	44 F5
Ballickmoyler / Baile Mhic Mhaoilir	45 A3
Ballilogue	53 A3
Ballina / Béal an Átha Co Mayo / Maigh Eo	14 H5
Ballina Co Tipperary	42 H4
Ballina Co Westmeath	34 F1
Ballinaboy Co Cork	60 G5
Ballinaboy Co Galway	29 C2
Ballinabrackey / Buaile na Bréachmhaí	34 H2
Ballinabranagh	45 A4
Ballinaclash / An Chlais	46 F3
Ballinadee / Baile na Daibhche	68 F1
Ballinafad / Béal an Átha Fada	24 H1
Ballinagar / Béal na Glarr	34 G4
Ballinagleragh / Baile na gCléireach	16 G4
Ballinakill	44 G3
Ballinalack / Béal Átha na Leac	26 F5
Ballinalea	46 G2
Ballinalee / Béal Átha na Lao	26 E3
Ballinamallard / Béal Átha na Mallacht	17 B1
Ballinameen / Béal an Átha na Min	24 H2
Ballinamore / Béal an Átha na Móir	17 A5
Ballinascarty / Béal na Scairte	68 E2
Ballinasloe / Béal Átha na Sluaighe	33 A3
Ballinaspick	61 C2
Ballinbranagh	45 A4
Ballinclashet	68 G1
Ballinclay	53 D4
Ballincollig / Baile an Chollaigh	60 F4
Ballincor	43 B1
Ballincrea	53 A5
Ballincreeshig	60 G5
Ballincurrig / Baile an Churraigh	61 A3
Ballindaggan / Baile an Daingin	53 C2
Ballindangan	60 H1
Ballinderreen / Baile an Doirín	31 D5
Ballinderry / Baile an Doire Co Antrim / Aontroim	11 C5
Ballinderry / Baile an Doire Co Tipperary / Tiobraid Árann	43 A2
Ballindine / Baile an Daighin	23 D5
Ballindoon	16 E5
Ballindrait / Baile an Droichid	9 C2
Ballineanig	57 B1
Ballineen / Béal Átha Fhínín	67 D1
Ballinfull	15 D2
Ballingarrane	49 D2
Ballingarry / Baile an Gharraí Co Tipperary / Tiobraid Árann	52 F2
Ballingarry / Baile an Gharraí Co Tipperary / Tiobraid Árann	43 B2
Ballingarry / Baile an Gharraí Co Limerick / Luimneach	50 E3
Ballingeary / Béal Átha an Ghaorthaidh Co Mayo	59 B5
Ballinglen / Baile an Gleanna	14 F3
Ballinglen Co. Wicklow	46 E4
Ballingurteen	67 C2
Ballinhassig / Béal Átha an Cheasaigh	60 G5
Ballinillaun	32 E4
Ballinkillin	53 B1
Ballinleeny	50 E3
Ballinloghig	57 C1
Ballinlough / Baile an Locha Co Meath / An Mhí	27 A4
Ballinlough / Baile an Locha Co Roscommon / Ros Comáin	24 F4
Ballinluska	68 H1
Ballinmuck	25 D2
Ballinoroher	68 E2
Ballinphonta	40 F3
Ballinran / Baile an Raithin	20 E5
Ballinrannig	57 B1
Ballinree	43 B3
Ballinrobe / Baile an Róba	22 H5
Ballinruan / Baile an Ruáin	42 E3
Ballinskelligs / Baile an Sceilg	57 C5
Ballinspittle / Béal Átha an Spidéil	68 F2
Ballintober / Baile an Tobair Co Mayho / Maigh Eo	22 H4
Ballintober / Baile an Tobair Co Roscommon / Ros Comáin	24 H4
Ballintogher / Bailean Tóchair	16 E4
Ballintoy / Baile an Tuaighe	4 H2
Ballintra / Baile an tSratha	8 G5
Ballintubbert	45 A2
Ballinunty / Baile an Fhantaigh	52 E2
Ballinure / Baile an Lúir	51 D2
Ballinurra	52 F4
Ballinvarry	53 A3
Ballinveny	43 C4
Ballinvoher Co Cork	61 A1
Ballinvoher Co Cork	59 D5
Ballinvronig	68 F2
Ballitore / Béal Átha an Tuair	45 B2
Ballivor / Baile Íomhair	35 A1
Ballon / Balana	45 C5
Balloo	12 F5
Balloor	16 E1
Ballsmill / Baile an gCléireach	19 A5
Ballure	8 F5
Ballyadack	60 H1
Ballyagran / Béal Átha Grean	50 E4
Ballyallinan	49 D3
Ballybaun	53 B2
Ballybay / Béal Átha Beithe	18 G4
Ballybeg Co Tipperary	43 C4
Ballybeg / An Baile Beag Co Tipperary / Tiobraid Árann	51 D5
Ballyboden / Baile Baodáin	36 F4
Ballybofey / Bealach Feich	9 A2
Ballyboggan	35 A2
Ballyboghil	36 F1
Ballybogy / Baile an Bhogaigh	4 G3
Ballybornia	33 D2
Ballybowler	57 C1
Ballyboy	34 E5
Ballybrack Co Kerry	57 D5
Ballybrack Co Kildare	35 C3
Ballybrack Co Waterford	61 C3
Ballybristy	43 C5
Ballybrittas / Baile Briotais	44 H1
Ballybrood	50 H2
Ballybrophy / Baile Uí Bhróithe	44 E3
Ballybroughan	42 E5
Ballybryan	34 H3
Ballybunnion / Baile an Bhuinneánaigh	48 G2
Ballyburn	45 B3
Ballycahane	42 H5
Ballycahill / Bealach Achaille	51 C1
Ballycallan	52 G1
Ballycanew / Baile Uí Chonnmhaí	54 F1
Ballycar	42 F5
Ballycarney / Baile Uí Chearnaigh	53 D2
Ballycarry / Baile Cora	12 F2
Ballycashin	62 H1
Ballycastle / Baile an Chaistil Co Antrim / An Aontroim	5 D2
Ballycastle Co Mayo	14 G3
Ballyclare / Bealach Cláir	11 D2
Ballyclogh / Baile Cloch	60 E1
Ballycogly	54 E5
Ballycolla / Baile Cholla	44 F3
Ballycolman	61 B3
Ballycommon / Baile Uí Chomáin	43 A3
Ballycomy	44 H4
Ballyconneely / Baile Conaola	29 C2
Ballyconnell / Béal Átha Conaill	17 B5
Ballycotton / Baile Choitín	61 B5
Ballycrossaun / Baile Crosáin	33 A5
Ballycroy / Baile Chruaich	13 D5
Ballycullane Co Waterford	62 E2
Ballycullane / Baile Uí Choiléain Co Wexford / Loch Garman	53 B5
Ballycullen	46 G2
Ballycumber / Béal Átha Chomair	34 E3
Ballydague	60 G2
Ballydangan / Baile Daighean	33 B3
Ballydavid Co Cork	61 35
Ballydavid / Baile an nGall Co Kerry / Ciarraí	57 B1
Ballydavis	44 H1
Ballydehob / Béal an Dá Chab	66 H3
Ballydeloughy	60 H1
Ballydesmond / Baile Deasumhan	59 B1
Ballydonegan	65 D2
Ballydoogan	32 G5
Ballydoyle	60 G1
Ballyduff / An Baile Dubh Co Kerry / Ciarraí	48 G3
Ballyduff / An Baile Dubh Co Kerry / Ciarraí	57 D1
Ballyduff / An Baile Dubh Co Waterford / Port Láirge	62 G1
Ballyduff / An Baile Dubh Co Waterford / Port Láirge	61 B2
Ballyduff / An Baile Dubh Co Wexford	54 E1
Ballyea	50 E2
Ballyeafy	61 B1
Ballyeaston / Baile Uistín	11 D2
Ballyeighan	43 C2
Ballyeighter	32 H4
Ballyeightragh	57 B1

Ballyfarnagh / Bealach Fearna 23 D3
Ballyfarnan 16 F5
Ballyfasy 53 A4
Ballyfeard / Baile Feá Aird 68 H1
Ballyferriter / Baile an Fhairtéaraigh 57 B1
Ballyfin / An Baile Fionn 44 F1
  Co Laois / Laois
Ballyfin / An Baile Fionn 54 F1
  Co Wexford / Loch Garman
Ballyforan / Béal Átha Feorainne 33 A2
Ballyfore 34 H3
Ballyfoyle 44 H5
Ballygalley / Baile Geithligh 12 E1
Ballygar / Béal Átha Ghártha 32 H1
Ballygarran Co Waterford 62 F2
Ballygarrett / Baile Ghearóid 54 F2
Ballygarries 23 C4
Ballygarvan / Baile Garbháin 60 G5
Ballygawley / Baile Uí Dhálaigh 16 E4
  Co Sligo / Sligeach
Ballygawley / Baile Uí Dhálaigh 18 F1
  Co Tyrone / Tir Eoghain
Ballygeana 51 A4
Ballygelly 11 D1
Ballyglass / An Baile Glas 24 F2
  Co Mayo / Maigh Eo
Ballyglass / An Baile Glas 14 G3
  Co Mayo / Maigh Eo
Ballyglass / An Baile Glas 23 C4
  Co Mayo / Maigh Eo
Ballyglass West 24 G3
Ballygorey 52 H5
Ballygortin 54 F2
Ballygowan / Baile Mhic Gabhann 12 F5
Ballygrady 60 E1
Ballygriffin 51 C2
Ballygub 53 A3
Ballygubba 50 F3
Ballyguyroe North 50 G5
Ballyhack 53 B5
Ballyhaght 50 F5
Ballyhahill / Baile Dhá Thuile 49 B2
Ballyhaise / Béal Átha hÉis 17 D5
Ballyhalbert / Baile Thalbóid 12 H5
Ballyhale / Baile Héil 31 C2
  Co Galway / Gaillimh
Ballyhale / Baile Héil 52 H3
  Co Kilkenny / Cill Chainnigh
Ballyhank 60 F5
Ballyhar / Baile Uí Aichir 58 H2
Ballyhaunis / Béal Átha hAmhnais 24 F4
Ballyhean / Bal Átha hÉine 22 H3
Ballyhear 31 D1
Ballyheelan / Bealach an Chaoláin 26 G3
Ballyheige / Baile Uí Thaidhg 48 F4
Ballyhenry 31 C1
Ballyhickey 42 E4
Ballyhoge / Baile Uí Cheog 53 D3
Ballyhomuck 52 H4
Ballyhoolahan 59 D1
Ballyhooly / Baile Átha hUlla 60 H2
Ballyhornan / Baile Uí Chornáin 20 G2
Ballyhugh Co Cavan 17 B5
Ballyhugh Co Offaly 34 H4
Ballyieragh 66 H4
Ballyjamesduff / Baile Shéamais Dhuibh 26 H2
Ballykean 34 G4
Ballykeel / An Baile Caol 19 D1
Ballykeeran / Bealach Caorthainn 33 C2

Ballykelly / Baile Uí Cheallaigh 3 D4
Ballykilleen 34 H4
Ballykilty 61 C4
Ballykinsella 63 B3
Ballyknockan 46 E1
Ballylanders / Baile an Londraigh 61 B5
  Co Cork / Corcaigh
Ballylanders / Baile an Londraigh 50 H4
  Co Limerick / Luimneach
Ballylaneen 62 G1
Ballylangley 68 F1
Ballyleague 25 B5
Ballyleen 62 G1
Ballyleny 19 A2
Ballylesson / Baile na Leasán 12 E5
Ballylickey 67 A1
Ballyliffin / Baile Lifin 3 A2
Ballyline 52 F2
Ballylinnen 44 H4
Ballylintagh 4 F4
Ballylongford / Baile Átha Longfoirt 49 A2
Ballylooby / Beala Átha Lúbaigh 50 H3
  Co Tipperary / Tiobraid Á;rannn
Ballylooby / Beala Átha Lúbaigh 51 C5
  Co Tipperary / Tiobraid Árann
Ballylucas 54 E3
Ballylumford 12 F1
Ballylynan / Baile Uí Laigheanáin 45 A3
Ballymacarbry / Baile Mhac Cairbre 51 D5
Ballymacaw / Baile Mhac Dháith 63 B4
Ballymacelligot 48 H5
Ballymachugh 26 G3
Ballymackey / Baile Uí Mhacai 43 B3
Ballymacmague 62 E2
Ballymacoda / Baile Mhac Óda 61 C4
Ballymacurly / Baile Mhic Thorlaigh 25 A4
Ballymacward / Baile Mhic an Bhaird 32 G3
Ballymagan / Baile Mhic Cionaoith 3 A3
Ballymagaraghy 3 D2
Ballymagorry / Baile Mhic Gofraidh 9 C1
Ballymahon / Baile Ui Mhatháin 33 D1
Ballymakeery / Baile Mhic Íre 59 C4
Ballymakenny 28 E3
Ballymanagh 32 F5
Ballymanus 26 G4
Ballymaquiff 42 E1
Ballymartin / Baile Mhic Grolla Mhártain 20 E5
Ballymartle 68 G1
Ballymena / An Baile Meanach 11 C1
Ballymoe / Béal Átha Mó 24 G4
Ballymoney / Baile Muine 4 G4
Ballymore Co Cork 61 A5
Ballymore / An Baile Mór 2 F3
  Co Donegal / Dún na nGall
Ballymore / An Baile Mór 34 E2
  Co Westmeath / An Iarmhí
Ballymore Eustace 35 D5
Ballymorris 62 H1
Ballymote / Baile an Mhóta 15 D5
Ballymount 45 C1
Ballymurphy / Baile Uí Mhurchu 53 B2
Ballymurragh 49 C4
Ballymurray / Baile Uí Mhuirigh 25 B5
Ballynabola 53 B4
Ballynabucky 32 E5
Ballynacally / Baile na Caillí 41 C5
Ballynacarriga / Béal na Carraige 67 C1
Ballynacarrigy / Baile an Carraige 34 F1
Ballynacarrow / Baile na Cora 15 D4

Ballynaclogh 43 B4
Ballynacole 61 B4
Ballynacorra 61 A4
Ballynacourty Co Waterford 62 F2
Ballynacourty Co Cork 68 G1
Ballynacree 26 H3
Ballynafid 26 G5
Ballynagaul Co Cork 60 H4
Ballynagaul Co Waterford 62 E3
Ballynagore / Béal Átha na nGabhar 34 F3
Ballynagree 59 D3
Ballynagrumoolia 60 G5
Ballynaguilkee 61 D1
Ballynahinch / Baile na hInse 20 E1
  Co Down / An Dún
Ballynahinch / Baile na hInse 42 H5
  Co Tipperary / Tiobraid Árann
Ballynahown Co Clare 40 F1
Ballynahown / Baile na hAbhann 30 F4
  Co Galway / Gaillimh
Ballynahown / Buaile na hAbhann 33 C3
  Co Westmeath / Anb Iarmhí
Ballynahulla 59 B1
Ballynakill Co Carlow 53 B1
Ballynakill Co Offaly 34 H4
Ballynakill Co Westmeath 33 C2
Ballynakilla 66 F2
Ballynamallaght 9 D2
Ballynamona / Baile an Móna 60 F2
  Co Cork / Corcaigh
Ballynamona Co Galway 33 A3
Ballynamona Co Wexford 53 C5
Ballynamuddagh 60 H2
Ballynamult / Beal na Molt 61 D1
Ballynana 57 C1
Ballynarry 26 G3
Ballynaskreena 48 G3
Ballynastangford / Baile na Stanfard 23 D4
Ballyneaner / Baile an Aonfhir 10 E1
Ballyneety / Baile an Fhaoitigh 50 G1
Ballyneill / Baile Uí Néill 52 F4
Ballynennan 52 F2
Ballynoe / An Baile Nua 61 B3
  Co Cork / Corcaigh
Ballynoe Co Galway 32 H4
Ballynure / Baile an Iuir 12 E2
Ballyorgan / Baile Uí Argáin 50 G5
Ballyoughter 54 F1
Ballyourane 67 A2
Ballypatrick / Baile Phádraig 52 E4
Ballyporeen / Béal Átha Póirín 51 B5
Ballyquin Co Kerry 47 D5
Ballyquin Co Waterford 52 G5
Ballyragget / Béal Átha Ragad 44 G4
Ballyrashane 4 F3
Ballyre 61 B3
Ballyreagh 18 F1
Ballyregan 68 G1
Ballyroan / Baile Átha an Róine 44 G3
Ballyroddy 25 A3
Ballyroe 47 C5
Ballyroebuck 53 D1
Ballyronan / Baile Uí Rónáin 11 A3
Ballyroney / Baile Uí Ruanai 19 D3
Ballyroon 66 F3
Ballyryan 45 B5
Ballysadare / Baile Easa Dara 15 D4
Ballyshannon / Béal Átha Seanaidh 8 F5
Ballysheen 48 G4

Ballyshoneen	63	B3
Ballyshrule	42	H1
Ballyskeagh	11	D5
Ballysloe	52	E1
Ballysorrell	43	D4
Ballysteen	49	D1
Ballyvaghan / *Baile Uí Bheacháin*	40	H1
Ballyvaldon	54	F3
ballyvalode	51	A2
Ballyvaloon	60	F3
Ballyveal	45	B5
Ballyveera	51	C5
Ballyvisteen	50	H5
Ballyvoge / *Baile Uí Bhuaigh*	66	F4
Ballyvoneen	32	H2
Ballyvonnavaun	41	D4
Ballyvorane	68	H1
Ballyvourney / *Baile Bhuirne*	59	B4
Ballyvoy / *Baile Bhóidh*	5	D2
Ballywalter / *Baile Bháltair*	12	H5
Ballyward / *Baile Mhic an Bhaird*	19	D3
Ballywildrick	4	E3
Ballywilliam Co Wexford	53	B3
Ballywilliam / *Baile Liam*	68	F2
Balnamore / *Béal an Átha Móir*	4	G4
Balrath / *Baile na Ratha*	28	E5
Balrothery	28	G5
Balscaddan	28	F5
Baltimore / *Dún na Séad*	67	A4
Baltinglass / *Bealach Conglais*	45	C3
Baltovin	48	G4
Baltray / *Baile Trá*	28	F4
Banada	15	B5
Banagher / *Beannchar*	33	C5
Banbridge / *Droichead na Banna*	19	C2
Bandon / *Droichead na Bandan*	68	E1
Banemore	48	H4
Bangor / *Beannachar* Co Down / *An Dún*	12	G3
Bangor / *Baingear* Co Mayo / *Maigh Eo*	13	D4
Banna	48	F4
Bannfoot	11	A5
Bansha Co Clare	41	C4
Bansha / *An Bháinseach* Co Tipperary / *Tiobraid Árann*	51	B3
Banteer / *Bántir*	59	D2
Bantry / *Beanntraí*	67	A2
Baranailt	3	D5
Barefield / *Gort Lomán*	41	D3
Barloge	67	A4
Barna / *Bearna* Co Galway / *Gaillimh*	31	C4
Barna Co Limerick	50	H2
Barna Co Offaly	43	C3
Barnacahoge	24	E2
Barnacawley	24	G3
Barnaderg / *Beara Dhearg*	32	F2
Barnagowlane	67	A1
Barnalisheen	43	D5
Barnalyra	24	E2
Barna Tra	13	D3
Barnycarroll / *Bearna Chearuill*	23	D4
Barrack Village	44	G5
Barraduff	59	A2
Barratoor	42	G1
Barrettstown	52	H3
Barrigone	49	C1
Barringtonsbridge	50	G1
Barrow	48	F5
Barry / *Barraigh*	25	D5
Bartlemy	61	A3
Bastardstown	64	E3
Batterstown / *Baile an Bhóthair*	35	D2
Baughna	34	G2
Baulbrack	59	C5
Baunskeha	52	H3
Bauntlieve	40	G3
Bawnaneel	59	C1
Bawnboy / *An Bábhún Búi* Co Cavan / *An Cabhán*	17	B5
Bawnboy Co Cork	67	A2
Bawnfune	51	D5
Bawnlahan	67	B4
Beagh	32	E1
Beal	48	G2
Bealaclugga / *Béal an Chloga*	40	H1
Bealadangan / *Béal an Daingin*	30	F3
Bealaha	40	E5
Bealin / *Béal Linne*	33	D2
Bealnablath	60	E5
Bealnamorive	60	E4
Beaufort / *Lios an Phúea*	58	G2
Bective	35	C1
Beenacouma	57	B2
Behernagh	60	H3
Bekan / *Béacán*	24	E4
Belcarra	22	H3
Belclare / *Béal Chláir*	31	D2
Belcoo / *Béal Cú*	16	H3
Belderg / *Béal Deirg*	14	E3
Belfast / *Béal Feiriste*	12	E4
Belgooly / *Béal Guala*	68	G1
Bellacorick / *Béal Átha Chomhraic*	14	E5
Belladrihid	15	D3
Bellagarvaun	22	E1
Bellaghy / *Baile Eachaidh*	11	A2
Bellahy	24	E1
Bellanacargy	17	D5
Bellanagare / *Béal Átha na gCarr*	24	H3
Bellananagh	26	F2
Bellanaleck / *Bealach na Leice*	17	B3
Bellanamullia / *Béal Átha na Muille*	33	B2
Bellaneeny	33	B3
Bellanode / *Béal Átha an Fhóid*	18	F3
Bellavary / *Béal Átha Bhearaigh*	23	C2
Belleek / *Béal Leice* Co Armagh / *Ard Mhacha*	19	A4
Belleek / *Béal Leice* Co Fermanagh / *Fear Manach*	16	G1
Bellewstown / *Baile an Bheileogaigh*	28	E5
Belmullet / *Béal an Mhuirthead*	13	C3
Beltoy	12	F2
Beltra Co Mayo	22	G1
Beltra / *Béal Trá* Co Sligo / *Sligeach*	15	C3
Belturbet / *Béal Tairbirt*	17	C5
Belvelly	60	H4
Benburb / *An Bhinn Bhorb*	18	H1
Bendooragh / *Bun Déurai*	4	G4
Bennettsbridge / *Droichead Binéid*	52	H2
Beragh / *Bearach*	10	E5
Berrings / *Biorainn*	60	F4
Bessbrook / *An Sruthán*	19	B4
Bettystown / *Baile an Bhiataigh*	28	F4
Bilboa / *Biolbó*	45	A4
Birdhill / *Cnocánan Éin Fhinn*	42	H5
Birr / *Biorra*	43	C1
Bishops Court	20	G2
Bishoppshall	52	H5
Black	61	B1
Black Bull	36	E2
Black Lion	34	E5
Blackcastle / *An Caisleán Dubh*	51	D3
Blackhall	53	D4
Blacklion / *An Blaic*	16	H3
Blackpool / *An Linn Dubh*	50	G4
Blackrock / *An Dúcharraig* Co Cork / *Corcaigh*	60	H4
Blackrock / *An Charraig Dhubh* Co Dublin / *Baile Átha Cliath*	36	G4
Blackrock / *Na Creagacha* Co Louth / *Lú*	28	E1
Blackwater / *An Abhainn Dubh*	54	F3
Blackwater Bridge	58	F5
Blackwatertown / *An Port Mór*	18	H1
Blackwood / *Coill Dubh*	35	B4
Blagh	4	F3
Blanchardstown / *Baile Bhlainséir*	36	E3
Blarney / *An Bhlarna*	60	G4
Bleary	19	B1
Blennerville / *Cathair Uí Mhóráin*	48	G5
Blessington / *Baile Coimín*	35	D5
Blue Ball / *An Phailís*	34	E5
Blueford	59	C1
Boardee	68	H1
Boardmills / *An Muileann Adhmaid*	20	E1
Bodyke / *Lúbám Dige*	42	G3
Bofeenaun	22	H1
Bog of the Ring	36	F1
Boggaun	43	D4
Boharboy	28	G1
Boher	50	G1
Boheraphuca	43	D2
Boherboy / *An Bóthar Buí* Co Cork / *Corcaigh*	59	C1
Bohereen	50	G1
Boherlahan / *An Bóthar Leathan*	51	C2
Bohermeen / *An Bóthar Mín*	27	B5
Bohernarnane	51	B4
Boherquill	26	F4
Boherroe	50	H2
Boho / *Botha*	17	A2
Bohola / *Both Chomhla*	23	D2
Bolea / *Both Liath*	4	E4
Boleran	4	F4
Boley Co Laois	45	A3
Boley Co Wicklow	45	D4
Boleyvogue	54	E2
Bolinglanna	21	D2
Boolakennedy	51	B4
Borris / *An Bhuiríos*	53	B1
Borris in Ossory / *Buiríos Mór Osrai*	44	E3
Borrisokane / *Buiríos Uí Chéin*	43	B2
Borrisoleigh / *Buiríos Ó Luigheach*	43	C5
Boston	41	D2
Bottomstown	50	G3
Bottomy	26	F5
Bouladuff / *An bhuaile Dhubh*	43	C5
Bovedy	4	F5
Bovevagh / *Boith Mhéabha*	3	D5
Boyle / *Mainistir na Búille*	25	A1
Boyounagh	24	F5
Brackagh	34	H4
Brackloon	24	H3
Bracklyn	34	H1
Bracknagh / *Breacánach* Co Offaly / *Uíbh Fhailí*	35	A5

Bracknagh Co Roscommon 25 B5
Brackny 33 D5
Brackwanshagh 14 G5
Brahalish 66 G2
Brandon / Cé Bhréanainn 47 D5
Brandum 18 F3
Brannockstown / Baile na mBreatnach 45 C1
Bray / Bré 36 G5
Bready / An Bhreadaigh 9 C1
Breaghna 67 D1
Breaghva 48 G1
Bree / Brí 53 D3
Breeda 61 C3
Brickeens / Na Broicíní 24 E4
Brideswell / Tobar Bride 33 B2
Bridge End / Ceann an Droichid 3 A4
Bridgeland 46 E4
Bridgetown Co Donegal 8 G4
Bridgetown / Baile an Droichid 64 E2
Brigh 10 H4
Brinlack 1 D3
Briska 62 F1
Brittas / An Briotás 36 E4
Broadford / Áth Leathan 49 D4
   Co Limerick / Luimneach
Broadford Co Kildare 35 A2
Broadway / Gráinseach Iúir 64 F3
Brockagh Co Londonderry 4 E5
Brockagh Co Wicklow 46 F2
Brookeborough / Achadh Lon 17 C2
Brookville 51 A3
Broomfield / Achadh an Bhrúim 18 H5
Brosna / Brosnach 49 B5
   Co Kerry / Ciarraí
Brosna / An Bhrosnach 43 C2
   Co Offaly / Uíbh Fhaili
Broughal 33 D5
Broughshane / Bruach 11 C1
Brownstown Co Kildare 35 B5
Brownstown Co Waterford 63 B4
Brownstown Co. Meath 27 D5
Bruckana 44 E5
Bruckless 8 E4
Bruff / An Brú 50 G3
Bruree / Brú Rí 50 F3
Bryansford / Áth Bhriain 20 E3
Buckna 11 D1
Buckode 16 F1
Bulgaden / Builgidin 50 G4
Bullaun 32 G4
Bunacurry 21 C1
Bunane 58 H5
Bunaw 58 F5
Bunbeg / An Bun Beag 1 D4
Bunbrosna / Bun Brosnaí 26 F5
Bunclody / Bun Clóidí 53 D1
Buncrana / Bun Cranncha 3 A3
Bundoran / Bun Dobhráin 16 F1
Bunglasha 58 E3
Bunlahy 26 E3
Bunmahon / Bun Machan 62 G2
Bunnafollistran 31 C1
Bunnaglass 42 F1
Bunnahown 13 C4
Bunnanaddan / Bun an Fheadáin 15 D5
Bunnyconnellan / Muine Chonalláin 15 A5
Bunratty 42 E5
Burnchurch 52 G2
Burncourt / An Chúirt Dóite 51 B5
Burnfoot / Bun na hAbhann 3 A4

Burnfort / Ráth an Tóiteáin 60 F2
Burren / Boirinn 31 C5
   Co Clare / An Clár
Burren / Boirinn 40 H5
   Co Clare / An Clár
Burren / Boirinn 19 C4
   Co Down / An Dún
Burrenfadda 40 G5
Burtonport / Ailt an Chorráin 1 C5
Bushmills / Muileann na Buaise 4 G2
Butler's Bridge 17 D5
Butlerstown / Baile an Bhuitléaraigh 68 E3
Buttevant / Cill na Mallach 60 F1
Bweeng 60 F3

C

Cabragh / An Chabrach 10 G5
Cadamstown / Baile Mhic Ádaim 35 A3
   Co Kildare / Cill Dara
Cadamstown / Baile Mhic Ádaim 44 E1
   Co Offaly / Uíbh Fhailí
Caheny 4 F5
Caher / An Chathair 42 F2
   Co Clare / An Clár
Caher Co Cork 66 F3
Caher Co Tipperary 51 C4
Caheracruttera 58 E1
Caheradrine 32 E4
Caheragh 67 A2
Caherakillen 32 G4
Caherbarnagh / An Chatair 57 D5
Caherconlish / Cathair Chinn Lis 50 G2
Caherconnell 40 H2
Caherdaniel / Cathair Dónall 65 D1
Caherea 40 H5
Caherlistrane / Cathair Loistréain 31 D2
Cahermore / Cathair Mhor 65 D2
   Co Cork / Corcaigh
Cahermore Co Galway 42 E1
Cahermuckee 67 A1
Cahermurphy 40 F5
Caherogan 40 F4
Caherphuca 32 E2
Cahersiveen / Cathair Saidhbhín 57 C4
Caim 53 C2
Caledon / Cionn Aird 18 G2
Callan / Callain 52 G2
Callow / An Caladh 23 D1
   Co Mayo / Maigh Eo
Callow Co Roscommon 24 H2
Caltra / An Cheatrach 32 H2
Caltraghlea 32 H3
Calverstown / Baile an Chalbhaigh 45 C1
Camira 43 B3
Camlough / Camloch 19 B4
Camolin / Cam Eolaing 54 E1
Camp / An Com 58 E1
Campile / Ceann Poill 53 B5
Camross / Camros 44 E2
Camus 30 F3
Canningstown / Baile Chainin 27 A1
Cape Castle 4 H3
Cappagh Co Cork 60 H2
Cappagh Co Limerick 50 E2
Cappagh / An Chapóg 10 F5
   Co Tyrone / Tir Eoghain
Cappagh White / An Cheapach 51 A2
Cappaghmore 41 D1

Cappagowlan 34 E5
Cappalinnan 44 E4
Cappamore / An Cheapach Mhór 50 H1
Cappataggle / Ceapaigh an tSeagail 32 H4
Cappeen 59 D5
Cappoquin / Ceapach Choinn 61 D2
Caran 24 H4
Carbury / Cairbre 35 A3
Carker 59 A1
Carland / Domhnach Carr 10 G5
Carlanstown / Droichead Chearballáin 27 B4
Carlingford / Cairlinn 19 C5
Carlow / Ceatharlach 45 B4
Carn Co Londonderry 10 G1
Carn Co Westmeath 34 E2
Carna / Carna 29 D3
Carnagh / Carranach 18 H4
Carnalbanagh 11 D1
Carnalbanagh Sheddings 11 D1
Carnanreagh 10 E1
Carnaross 27 A4
Carncastle 12 E1
Carndonagh / Carn Domhnach 3 B2
Carnew / Carn an Bhua 46 E5
Carney / Fearann Uí Chearnaigh 15 D2
   Co Sligo / Sligeach
Carney / Carnaigh 43 A2
   Co Tipperary / Tiobraid Árann
Carnlough / Carnlach 6 E5
Carnmoney / Carn Monaidh 12 E3
Carnteel / Carn tSiail 18 F1
Carracastle / Ceathrú an Chaisil 24 F1
Carragh / Céarach 35 C4
Carraghs 24 G4
Carraholly / Ceathrú Chalaidh 22 F3
Carran / An Carn 40 H2
   Co Clare / An Clár
Carran Co Kilkenny 52 H1
Carraroe / An Cheathrú Rua 30 F4
Carrick / An Charraig 7 C4
Carrick / An Charraig 53 C5
Carrick-on-Shannon / Cora Droma Rúisc 25 B1
Carrick-on-Suir / Carraig na Siúire 52 F4
Carrickaboy / Carraigigh Bhuí 26 G2
Carrickart / Carraig Airt 2 G3
Carrickashedoge 27 C2
Carrickboy / An Charraig Bhuí 26 E5
Carrickfergus / Carraig Fhearghais 12 F3
Carrickmacross / Carraig Mhachaire 27 C1
Carrickmines / Carraig Mhaighin 36 G4
Carrickmore or Termon Rock / 10 F4
   An Charraig Mhór
Carrickroe 18 F2
Carrig 43 C1
Carrigaday 48 E5
Carrigagulla 59 D3
Carrigaholt / Carraig an Chnabhaltaigh 48 G1
Carrigahorig / Carraig an Chomhraic 43 B1
Carrigaline / Carraig Uí Leighin 60 H5
Carrigallen / Carraig Álainn 26 E1
Carrigan / An Carraigín 26 F2
Carriganimmy / Carraig an Ime 59 C3
Carriganroe 51 B5
Carrigans / An Carraigin 3 A5
Carrigatogher / Carraig an Tóchair 42 H4
Carriggower 46 G1
Carrigkerry 49 C3
Carrignavar / Carraig na bhFear 60 G3
Carrigtohill / Carraig Thuathail 61 A4
Carrow 51 B2

Carrowdore / *Ceathrú Dobhair* 12 G4
Carrowduff Co Clare 40 F2
Carrowduff Co Roscommon 24 H4
Carroweden 15 C4
Carrowkeel / *An Cheathrú Chaol* 2 H3
  Co Donegal / *Dún na nGall*
Carrowkeel Co Galway 32 G5
Carrowkeel Co Mayo 22 H5
Carrowkeelanahglass 24 F5
Carrowmenagh 3 C2
Carrowmore Co Galway 31 D5
Carrowmore / *Ceathrú Mhór Laecan* 14 G3
  Co Mayo / *Maigh Eo*
Carrowmore Co Mayo 23 D5
Carrowmore Co Sligo 15 C5
Carrowmoreknock 31 C2
Carrownacon 23 C4
Carrowpadeen 15 A3
Carrowreagh 33 A3
Carrowrory 33 C1
Carrowteige 13 D2
Carryduff / *Ceathrú Aedha Dhuibh* 12 E5
Cashel Co Carlow 53 B1
Cashel Co Laois 44 G2
Cashel Co Galway 30 E2
Cashel / *Caiseal* 51 C2
  Co Tipperary / *Tiobraid Árann*
Cashelgarran / *Caiseal an Ghearráin* 15 D2
Cashla 32 E3
Cassagh 53 B4
Castlebaldwin /
  Béal Átha an gCarraigíní 16 E5
Castlebar / *Caisleán an Bharraigh* 22 H2
Castlebellingham /
  Baile an Ghearlánaigh 28 E2
Castleblakeney / *Gallach* 32 G2
Castleblayney / *Baiule na Lorgan* 18 H5
Castlebridge /
  Droichead an Cháisleéain 54 E4
Castlecat / *Caiseal Cait* 4 G3
Castlecaulfield / *Baile Uí Dhonnaile* 10 G5
Castlecomer / *Caisleán an Chomair* 44 H4
Castleconnell / *Caisleán Uí Chonaill* 42 G5
Castleconor 14 H4
Castlecoote 25 A5
Castlecor / *Caisleán na Cora* 60 E1
Castle Cove 57 D5
Castlecuffe 34 E5
Castledawson / *An Seanmhullach* 11 A2
Castlederg / *Caisleán na Deirge* 9 B3
Castledermot / *Diseart Diarmada* 45 B3
Castledockrell 53 D2
Castleellis 54 E3
Castlefinn / *Caisleán na Finne* 9 B2
Castlefreke 67 D3
Castlegal 16 E1
Castlegregory / *Caisleán Ghriaire* 48 E5
Castlehill / *Caorthannán* 22 E1
  Co Mayo / *Maigh Eo*
Castlhill Co Mayo 14 G5
Castleisland / *Oileán Ciarraí* 59 A1
Castlejordan / *Caisleán Shuirdáin* 34 H3
Castleknock / *Caisleán Cnucha* 36 E3
Castleleiny / *Caisleán Laighnigh* 43 D4
Castlelyons / *Caisleán Ó Liatháin* 61 A2
Castlemaine / *Caisleán na Mainge* 58 G1
Castlemartyr / *Baile na Martra* 61 B4
Castleplunket / *Lois Lachna* 24 H4
Castlepollard / *Baile na gCros* 26 G4

Castlequarter 31 D3
Castlequin 57 C3
Castlerahan 26 H3
Castlerea / *An Caisleán Riabhach* 24 G3
Castlereagh 12 E4
Castlerock / *Carraig Ceasail* 4 E3
Castleshane / *Caisleán an tSiáin* 18 G3
Castletown Co Clare 40 H2
Castletown /
  Baile Chaisleáin Chinn Eich 67 D1
  Co Cork / *Corcaigh*
Castletown / *Baile an Chaisleáin* 44 F2
  Co Laois / *Laois*
Castletown / *Baile an Chaisleáin* 50 E3
  Co Limerick / *Luimneach*
Castletown / *Baile an Chaisleáin* 27 C3
  Co Meath / *An Mhí*
Castletown / *Baile an Chaisleáin* 26 G4
  Co Westmeath / *An Iarmhí*
Castletown / *Baile an Chaisleáin* 46 G5
  Co Wexford / *Loch Garman*
Castletown Bearhaven 66 E2
Castletown Geoghegan 34 F2
Castletownroche /
  Baile Chaisleáin an Róistigh 60 G1
Castletownshend / *Baile an Chaisleáin* 67 B3
Castleville 23 D5
Castlewarren / *Caisleán an Bhairinnigh* 45 A5
Castlewellan / *Caisleán Uidhilín* 20 E3
Causeway / *An Tóchar* 48 G3
Cavan / *An Cabhán* 26 G1
Cavangarden 8 F5
Caves 51 B5
Ceancullig 67 B2
Cecilstown / *Baile an Bhriotaigh* 60 B2
Cecilstown / *Baile an Bhriotaigh* 60 E1
Celbridge / *Cill Droichid* 35 D3
Chanonrock 27 D1
Chapel 53 C3
Chapeltown / *Baile an tSéipéil* 20 G2
  Co Down / *An Dún*
Chapeltown / *An Caol* 57 B4
  Co Kerry / *Ciarraí*
Charlemont 18 H1
Charlestown / *Baile Chathail* 24 E1
Cheekpoint / *Pointe na Síge* 53 A5
Cherryville 35 A5
Chesney's Corner 11 B2
Church Cross / *Cnoc na Rátha* 67 A3
Church Hill / *Min an Lábáin* 2 F5
  Co Donegal / *Dún na nGall*
Church Hill / *An Droim Meánach* 9 A4
  Co Tyrone / *Tir Eoghain*
Church Hill 48 F5
Church Town / *Tulaigh an Iúir* 3 A5
Churchboro Cross 33 B1
Churchfield 22 G5
Churchstreet 24 H2
Churchtown / *Baile an Teampaill* 50 F5
  Co Cork / *Corcaigh*
Churchtown / *Baile an Teampaill Theas* 61 B5
  Co Cork / *Corcaigh*
Churchtown Co Wexford 64 G3
Churchtown Co Wexford 63 C4
Clabby / *Clabaigh* 17 D1
Claddaghduff / *An Cladach Dubh* 29 B1
Clady Co Londonderry 11 A1
Clady / *Clóidigh* 9 B2
  Co Tyrone / *Tír Eoghain*
Cladymilltown / *Baile an Mhuillinn* 19 A3

Claggan 22 E1
Clane / *Claonadh* 35 C4
Clara / *Cióirtheach* 34 E3
Clarahill 34 F5
Clare / *An Clár* 19 B2
Clarecastle / *Droichead an Chláir* 41 D4
Clareen / *An Cláirin* 43 D1
Claregalway / *Baile Chláir* 31 D3
Claremorris / *Clár Chlainne Mhuiris* 23 D4
Clarina / *Clár Aidhne* 50 F1
Clarinbridge / *Droichead an Chláirin* 32 E4
Clash 43 B3
Clash North 49 B3
Clash South 49 B3
Clashdrumsmith 51 A3
Clashmore / *Clais Mhór* 61 D3
Clashroe 52 G5
Claudy / *Clóidigh* 10 E1
Clawinch 25 B5
Cleggan / *An Cloigeann* 29 C1
Clenagh 41 D5
Clerragh 24 G3
Cleristown 53 D5
Clifden / *An Clochán* 29 C1
Clifferna / *An Chliaifearna* 26 H1
Cliffony / *Cliafuine* 16 E1
Clogga Co Kilkenny 52 H5
Clogga Co Wicklow 46 G5
Clogh / *An Chloch* 4 H5
  Co Antrim / *Aontriom*
Clogh Co Kilkenny 44 H4
Clogh Co Laois 44 F3
Clogh Co Limerick 49 D2
Clogh Co Wexford 54 F1
Clogh Mills / *Muileann na Cloiche* 4 H5
Cloghan / *An Clochan* 8 H2
  Co Donegal / *Dún na nGall*
Cloghan Co Offaly 33 C5
Cloghan Co Westmeath 34 H1
Cloghane Co Cork 66 F4
Cloghane / *An Chlochan* 47 D5
  Co Kerry / *Ciarraí*
Cloghaun Co Clare 40 F5
Cloghaun Co Galway 31 C3
Cloghaun Co Galway 31 D3
Cloghboley / *Clochbhuile* 15 D2
Cloghbrack / *An Chloch Bhreac* 30 G1
  Co Galway / *Gaillimh*
Cloghbrack Co Meath 35 A1
Cloghcor 9 C1
Clogheen / *An Chloichín* 51 D5
  Co Tipperary / *Tiobraid Árann*
Clogheen Co Waterford 51 C5
Clogher Co Mayo 13 B4
Clogher / *An Clochar* 22 G3
  Co Mayo / *Maigh Eo*
Clogher Co Mayo 22 H4
Clogher Co Roscommon 25 B2
Clogher / *Clochar* 18 E1
  Co Tyrone / *Tir Eoghain*
Cloghera 42 F5
Clogherhead / *Ceann Chlochair* 28 F3
Cloghfin 10 F5
Cloghjordan / *Cloch Shiurdáin* 43 B3
Cloghmore / *An Chloich Mhoir* 21 D2
Cloghpook 44 H5
Cloghran / *Clochrán* 36 F2
Cloghvoula 49 B5
Cloghy / *Clochaigh* 20 H1
Clohamon / *Cloch Amainn* 53 D1

Clogharinka Co Offaly	35 A3	
Clogharinka Co Kilkenny	44 H5	
Clohernagh	63 B3	
Clologe	54 E1	
Clomantagh	44 F5	
Clonakenny / Cluain Uí Chionaoith	43 D3	
Clonakilty / Cloich na Coillte	67 D2	
Clonalea	43 B4	
Clonalvy / Cluain Ailbhe	28 E5	
Clonard Co Cork	61 C4	
Clonard / Cluain Ioraird	35 A2	
Co Meath / An Mhí		
Clonard Great	54 E5	
Clonascra	33 C3	
Clonaslee / Cluain na Slí	34 F5	
Clonavoe	34 H4	
Clonbern / Cluain bheirn	32 F1	
Clonbulloge / Cluain Bolg	35 A4	
Clonbur / An Fhairche	30 G1	
Cloncagh / Cluain Cath	49 D3	
Cloncrave	34 H2	
Cloncreen	34 H4	
Cloncullen	34 E1	
Cloncully	44 E2	
Clondalkin / Clauin Dolcáin	36 E3	
Clondrohid	59 C4	
Clondulane	61 A2	
Clonea / Clauin Fhia	52 F5	
Clonee / Cluain Aodha	36 E2	
Cloneen Co Offaly	34 G3	
Cloneen / An Cluainín	52 E3	
Co Tipperary / Tiobraid Árann		
Clonegall / Cluain na nGall	45 D5	
Clonelly	9 A5	
Clones / Cluain Eois	18 E4	
Clonfert / Cluain Fearta	33 B4	
Clongeen	53 C5	
Clonincurragh	44 F2	
Clonkeen	44 G2	
Clonkeen Co Kerry	59 A3	
Clonkeenkerrill	32 F3	
Clonlost / Cluain Loiste	34 H1	
Clonmacnoise	33 C3	
Clonmany / Cluain Maine	3 A2	
Clonmeen	44 E4	
Clonmel / Cluain Meala	52 E4	
Clonmellon / Ráistín	27 A5	
Clonmore / Cluain Mhór	45 D4	
Co Carlow / Ceatharlach		
Clonmore Co Louth	28 F3	
Clonmore Co Tipperary	43 D4	
Clonmult	61 B3	
Clonony	33 C4	
Clonroche / Cluain an Róistigh	53 C3	
Clonsilla / Cluain Saileach	36 E3	
Clontarf / Cluain Tarbh	36 F3	
Clontibret / Cluain Tiobrad	18 G4	
Clontubbrid	44 F5	
Clonycavan	35 A1	
Clonygowan / Cluain na nGamham	34 G5	
Clonyquin	34 G5	
Cloonacauneen	31 D4	
Cloonacool / Cluain na Cúile	15 B5	
Cloonagh	26 F3	
Cloonbrennaun	24 G5	
Clooncah	25 B5	
Cloondaff	22 G1	
Cloondara / Cluain Dá Ráth	25 C4	
Cloone / An Chluain	25 D1	
Cloone Grange	25 D2	
Clooneagh	25 C3	
Clooneen	26 F3	
Clooney	8 E2	
Cloonfad Co Roscommon	24 F4	
Cloonfad / Cluain Fada	33 B4	
Co Roscommon / Ros Comáin		
Cloonfallagh / Cluain Falach	24 E3	
Cloonfeagh	40 H4	
Cloonfinish	24 E1	
Cloonfower	24 G3	
Cloonkeelaun	15 A4	
Cloonkeen Co Galway	24 G4	
Cloonkeen Co Mayo	22 H3	
Cloonkeen Co Roscommon	24 G5	
Cloonkeevy / Cluain Ciabhaigh	15 D5	
Cloonlara / Cluain Lára	42 G5	
Cloonlee	23 D3	
Cloonloogh / Cluain Lua	24 H1	
Cloonlusk	51 A2	
Cloonmurray	25 A4	
Cloonnacat	24 F5	
Cloonsheever	24 G3	
Cloontia / Na Cluainte	24 F1	
Cloontuskert	25 B4	
Cloonusker	42 G3	
Cloonycarney	15 A3	
Cloonymorris	32 H4	
Cloonyogan	25 A4	
Cloonyquin / Cluain Uí Choinn	25 A3	
Closh	44 E2	
Clough / An Chloch	20 F2	
Cloughduv	60 E5	
Cloverhill	17 D5	
Cloyne / Cluain	61 B5	
Coachford / Áth an Chóiste	60 E4	
Coagh / An Cuach	10 H4	
Coalbrook / Glaise an Ghuail	52 E1	
Coalisland / Oileán an Ghuail	10 H5	
Coan / An Cuan	44 H4	
Cobh / An Cóbh	61 A5	
Caddy	11 B2	
Colbinstown / Baile Choilbín	45 C2	
Colehill / Cnoc na Góla	26 E5	
Coleraine / Cúil Raithin	4 F3	
Colestown	53 D4	
Collinstown / Baile na gCailleach	26 H5	
Collon / Collan	27 D3	
Collooney / Cúil Mhuine	15 D4	
Colman	51 D3	
Colmanstown / Baile Uí Chlúmháin	32 F3	
Colp	28 F4	
Comber / An Comar	12 F5	
Commaun	43 B5	
Commons Co Cork	60 E5	
Commons / Na Coimíní		
Co Tipperary / Tiobraid Árann	52 F1	
Cong / Conga	30 H1	
Conlig / An Choinleic	12 G4	
Conna / Conaithe	61 B2	
Connemara	30 E2	
Connolly / Fioch Rua	40 G4	
Connor	11 C2	
Connonagh	67 C3	
Convoy / Conmhaigh	9 B1	
Cookstown / An Chorr Chriochach	10 H4	
Cool	61 C1	
Coolagary	34 H4	
Coolaney / Cúil Áine	15 D4	
Coolanheen	61 D2	
Coolattin	46 E5	
Coolbaun / An Cúl Bán		
Co Tipperary / Tiobraid Árann	43 A2	
Coolbaun / An Cúl Bán	44 H4	
Coolboy Co Donegal	2 G5	
Coolboy / An Cúl Buí	46 E5	
Co Wicklow / Cill Mhantáin		
Coolboy Co Tipperary	51 A5	
Coolderry / Cúl Doire	43 D2	
Coole / An Chuil	26 G4	
Coole Abbey	61 A2	
Coolea / Cúil Aodha	59 B4	
Coolea	60 H2	
Coolegreane	16 G4	
Coolgrange	52 H1	
Coolgreany / Cúil Chréine	46 F5	
Coolgreen	60 H3	
Coolinny	60 H2	
Coolmeen / Cúil Mhín	49 B1	
Coolnafarna	24 F4	
Coolnagun	26 F4	
Coolock	36 F3	
Coolrain / Cúil Ruáin	44 E2	
Coolroe	54 F2	
Coolross	43 B1	
Coolsallagh	60 H5	
Coolshaghtena	25 B5	
Coomleagh	67 B1	
Coonagh	50 F1	
Cooneen / An Cúinnín	17 D2	
Cooraclare / Cuar an Chláir	40 F5	
Coorleagh	45 A5	
Coosane	66 H3	
Cootehall / Uachtar Thíre	25 A1	
Cootehill / Muinchille	18 E5	
Coralstown / Baile Mhic Cearúill	34 H2	
Corbally Co Clare	40 E5	
Corbally / An Corrbhaile	14 A4	
Co Sligo / Sligeach		
Corclogh	13 B3	
Corcreeghagh	27 D1	
Corcullin	14 E5	
Cordal / Cordal	59 A1	
Cordarragh	22 F4	
Corduff / An Chorr Dubh	35 B4	
Cork / Corcaigh	60 G4	
Corkey / Corcaigh	4 H4	
Corlea	25 C5	
Corlee	23 D1	
Corlough	17 A5	
Cornafulla / Corr an Fola	33 B3	
Cornanagh	23 C4	
Corndarragh	34 F4	
Corrakyle	42 G2	
Corrandulla / Cor an Dola	31 D3	
Corraun	21 D2	
Correen	11 C1	
Corries Cross	53 B1	
Corrofin / Cora Finne	40 H3	
Co Clare / An Clár		
Corrofin Co Galway	32 E2	
Corrondher	50 E3	
Corry	16 G4	
Cortown / An Baile Corr	27 B4	
Corvoley	14 F4	
Costelloe / Casla	30 F4	
Coumduff	57 D1	
Countygate	61 A2	
Courthoyle	53 C4	
Courtmacsherry / Cúirt Mhic Shéafraidh	68 E1	
Courtmatrix	49 D3	

Courtown / *Baile na Cúirte* 54 F1
Cousane 67 B1
Coxtown 32 H4
Craan 46 E5
Craanford / *Áth an Chorráin* 46 E5
Crafield 46 F3
Craggagh 40 G1
Cragroe 42 E3
Craig 10 E2
Craigavad / *Creig an Bhada*
Craigavole 4 F5
Craigavon 19 B1
Craigs / *Na Creeaga* 11 B1
Cranagh / *An Chrannóg* 10 E2
Crane 54 E2
Cranford / *Creamhghort* 2 G3
Cranny / *An Chrannaigh* 40 G5
  Co Clare / *An Clár*
Cranny Co Londonderry 10 H3
Cratloe / *An Chreatalach* 42 E5
Craughwell / *Creachmhaoi* 32 F4
Crawfordsburn / *Sruth Chráfard* 12 F3
Crazy Corner 34 G1
Creagh Co Cork 67 A3
Creagh / *Créach* 17 C2
  Co Fermanagh / *Fear Manach*
Creaghanroe / *Crícheán Rua* 18 H4
Crecora / *Craobh Chomhartha* 50 F2
Creegh / *An Chrioch* 40 F5
Creeslough / *An Craoslach* 2 F3
Crettyard 44 H4
Creevagh 14 G3
Creeves 49 D2
Cregg Co Clare 30 H5
Cregg Co Cork 67 C3
Creggan Co Offaly 33 C4
Creggan / *An Creagán* 10 F4
  Co Tyrone / *Tír Eoghain*
Cregganbaun / *An Creagán Bán* 22 E4
Creggs / *Na Creaga* 24 H5
Crindle 3 D4
Crinkill / *Crionchoill* 43 C1
Croaghrimbeg 22 G4
Crockets Town 14 H4
Croghan / *Cruachán* 34 G3
Co Offaly / *Uibh Fhailí*
Croghan Co Roscommon 25 A2
Crolly 1 D5
Cromane / *An Cromán* 58 E2
Cromlin 17 A5
Crookedwood / *Tigh Munna* 26 G5
Crookhaven / *An Cruachán* 66 G4
Crookstown / *An Baile Gallda* 60 E5
  Co Cork / *Corcaigh*
Crookstown Co Kildare 45 B2
Croom / *Cromadh* 50 F2
Cross Barry / *Croisan Bharraigh* 60 F5
Cross Keys / *Carraig an Tobair* 26 G2
  Co Cavan / *An Cabhán*
Cross Keys Co Meath 26 H4
Cross Keys Co Meath 35 D1
Cross Mahon 68 E1
Cross Roads / *Na Croisbhealaí* 9 A2
Cross / *An Chrois* 48 F1
  Co Clare / *An Clár*
Crossabeg / *Na Crosa Beaga* 54 E4
Crossakeel / *Crosa Caoil* 27 A4
Crossboyne 23 D4
Crossconnell 33 A4
Crossdoney / *Cros Domhnaigh* 26 F1

Crossea 26 E5
Crosserlough / *Crois ar Loch* 26 G2
Crossgar / *An Chrois Ghearr* 20 F1
Crossgare 4 F4
Crosshaven / *Bun an Tábhairne* 60 H5
Crosskeys / *Na hEochracha* 45 A1
Crossmaglen / *Crois Mhic Lionnáin* 19 A5
Crossmolina / *Crois Mhaoilíona* 14 G5
Crossna 25 A1
Crossooha 31 D5
Crosspatrick / *Crois Phádraig* 44 E5
  Co Kilkenny / *Cill Chainnigh*
Crosspatrick Co Wicklow 46 E5
Crosswell 24 H5
Crowbally 61 B4
Crumlin / *Cromghlinn* 11 C4
Crumpane 66 E1
Crusheen / *Croisín* 41 D3
Crutt 44 H4
Cuilkillew 22 H1
Culcavy 19 D1
Culdaff / *Cúil Dabhcha* 3 C2
Culfadda 24 G1
Culkeeny 3 C1
Cullahill / *An Chúlchoill* 44 F4
Cullane 50 H4
Cullaville / *Baile Mhic Cullach* 18 H5
Culleen 42 E5
Culleens / *Na Coillíní* 15 A4
Cullen / *Cuillin* 59 C2
  Co Cork / *Corcaigh*
Cullen / *Cuilleann* 51 A2
  Co Tipperary / *Tiobraid Árann*
Cullenagh 50 H5
Cullenstown 63 D3
Cullin 23 D1
Cullybackey / *Coill na Baice* 11 B1
Cullyhanna / *Coilleach Eanach* 19 A4
Culnady / *Cúil Chnáidí* 10 H1
Cultra 12 E3
Currabeha / *An Chorr Bheithe* 61 B2
Curracloe / *Currach Cló* 54 E4
Curraclogh 59 D5
Curragh / *An Currach* 61 D4
Curragh West / *An Currach Thiar* 24 F5
Curragha 36 E1
Curraghalicky 67 C2
Curraghboy / *An Currach Buí* 33 B2
Curraghlawn 46 E4
Curraghmore 53 A3
Curraghroe / *An Currach Rua* 25 B4
Curraglass / *Cora Chlas* 61 B2
Curragunneen / *Currach Guinín* 43 D3
Curran / *An Corrán* 10 H2
Curranavilla 30 G4
Currans 58 H1
Curreeny / *Na Coirríní* 43 B5
Currow / *Corra* 58 H1
Curry / *An Choraidh* 24 E1
Curryglass 66 F2
Cushendall / *Bun Abhann Dalla* 6 E4
Cushendun / *Bun Abhann Duinne* 6 E3
Cushina 34 H5

Dalystown 34 G2
Damastown 36 F1
Damhead 4 F4
Danesfort / *Cún Feart* 25 D4
Dangandargan 51 C3
Darkley / *Dearclaigh* 18 H3
Dartry 18 F5
Davidstown / *Baile Dháith* 53 D3
Deerpark / *Páirc na bhFia* 31 C1
Delgany / *Deilgne* 36 G5
Delphi 22 E5
Delvin / *Dealbhna* 27 A5
Dernagree / *Doire na Graí* 59 C2
Derradda / *Doire Fhada* 17 A5
Derragh 40 H4
Derreen Co Clare 40 F3
Derreen Co Kerry 57 C4
Derreen / *Dan Doirín* 21 D2
  Co Mayo / *Maigh Eo*
Derreenacarrin 66 G1
Derreenard 67 A3
Derreenauliff 58 E5
Derreeny 66 F2
Derries Co Offaly 34 E4
Derries Co Offaly 35 A4
Derrineel 33 B3
Derrinturn 35 A3
Derryadd / *Doire Fhada* 11 B5
Derrybeg / *Doirí Beaga* 1 D4
Derryboy / *Doire Buí* 20 F1
Derrybrien / *Daraidh Braoin* 42 F1
Derrycanan 25 B4
Derryclogh 67 B2
Derrycon 44 F1
Derrycooly 34 E4
Derrydolney 33 D5
Derryfada 44 E5
Derrygareen 42 H5
Derrygile 44 G1
Derrygolan 34 F3
Derrygonnelly / *Doire Ó gConaíle* 17 A1
Derrygowna 25 C5
Derrygrath 51 C4
Derrygrogan 34 G4
Derrykeighan 4 G3
Derrylahan 33 B3
Derrylin / *Doire Loinn* 17 B4
Derryloughlin 58 E5
Derrymore 48 F5
Derrynacaheragh 67 B1
Derrynoose / *Doire Núis* 18 H3
Derryrush 30 E3
Derrywode 24 G4
Dervock / *Dearbhóg* 4 G3
Derryvoreada 30 E1
Desert 61 A3
Desertmartin / *Diseart Mhártain* 10 H2
Devenish / *Daimhinis* 17 B2
Dingle / *An Daingean* 57 C1
Doagh / *Dumhach* 11 D3
Dolla / *An Doladh* 43 A4
Dollingstown 19 C1
Dollymount / *Cnocán Doirinne* 36 G3
Donabate / *Domhnach Bat* 36 G1
Donacarney 28 F4
Donadea 35 C3
Donaghadee / *Domhnach Daoi* 12 G4
Donaghcloney / *Domhnach Cluana* 19 C1
Donaghmore / *Domhnach Mór* 44 E3
  Co Laois / *Laois*

D

Daingean / *An Daingean* 34 G4
Dalkey 36 G4

Donaghmore Co Meath	36 E1	
Donaghmore Co Tyrone	10 G5	
Donaghpatrick / *Domhnach Phádraig*	27 C4	
Donard Co Wexford	53 B3	
Donard / *Dún Ard*	45 D2	
Co Wicklow / *Cill Mhantáin*		
Donaskeagh	51 B2	
Donegal / *Dún na nGall*	8 G4	
Doneraile / *Dún ar Aill*	60 F1	
Donohill / *Dún eochaille*	51 B2	
Donore Co Meath	35 B1	
Donore / *Dún Uabhair*	28 E4	
Donoughmore / *Domhnach Mór*	60 E3	
Dooagh / *Dumha Acha*	21 C1	
Doocarrick	18 E5	
Doocastle / *Caisleán an Dumha*	24 F1	
Doocharry / *An Dúchoraidh*	8 F1	
Dooega / *Dumha Éige*	21 C2	
Doogary	26 E1	
Dooghbeg	21 D2	
Doogort	21 C1	
Doohamiat	18 G4	
Doohat / *Dúháite*	18 E5	
Doohooma / *Dumha Thuama*	13 C5	
Dooleeg	14 F5	
Doolieve	68 G1	
Doolin	40 F2	
Doon Co Galway	32 H3	
Doon / *Dún*	51 A1	
Co Limerick / *Luimneach*		
Doon Co Tipperary	61 B1	
Doona	13 C5	
Doonaha / *Dún Átha*	48 G1	
Doonbeg / *An Dún Beag*	40 E5	
Doonmanagh	57 D2	
Doonreaghan	29 D2	
Doornane	52 H5	
Dooyork	13 C5	
Dough	66 F4	
Doughiska	31 D4	
Douglas / *Dúglas*	60 G5	
Dovea / *Dubhfhéith*	43 C5	
Dowling	52 G4	
Downhill / *Dún Bó*	4 E3	
Downing	60 H1	
Downpatrick / *Dún Pádraig*	20 F2	
Dowra / *An Damhshraith*	16 G4	
Drangan / *Drongan*	52 E2	
Draperstown / *Baile na Croise*	10 G2	
Dreen	10 F1	
Dreenagh	48 E3	
Drehidasillagh	48 F5	
Driminidy	67 B2	
Drimmo	44 F2	
Drimoleague / *Drom Dhá Liag*	67 B2	
Drinagh / *Draighneagh*	67 C2	
Co Cork / *Corcaigh*		
Drinagh Co Galway	29 C2	
Drinagh Co Roscommon	25 C4	
Drinagh Co Wexford	54 E5	
Drinaghan	15 A3	
Dring / *Droing*	26 F3	
Dripsey / *An Druipseach*	60 E4	
Drogheda / *Droichead Átha*	28 E4	
Droichead Nua (Newbridge)	35 C5	
Drom Co Kerry	47 D5	
Drom / *An Drom*	43 C5	
Co Tipperary / *Tiobraid Árann*		
Dromagh	59 D2	
Dromahair / *Droim dhá Thiar*	16 F3	
Dromara / *Droim Bearach*	19 D2	
Dromaragh	57 D4	
Dromboy South	60 G3	
Dromcolliher / *Drom Collachair*	49 D4	
Dromcunnig	48 G4	
Dromgariff	60 G3	
Dromin Co Limerick	50 G3	
Dromin / *Droim Ing*	28 E3	
Co Louth / *Lú*		
Dromina / *Drom Aidhne*	50 E5	
Dromineer / *Drom Inbhir*	43 A3	
Dromiskin / *Droim Ineasclainn*	28 E2	
Drommahane / *Droim Átháin*	60 F2	
Drommin	22 F4	
Dromnea	66 G3	
Dromod / *Dromad*	25 C3	
Dromore west / *An Droim Mór Thiar*	15 B3	
Dromore / *Droim Mór*	19 D1	
Co Down / *An Dún*		
Dromore / *An Droim Mór*	9 C5	
Co Tyrone / *Tír Eoghain*		
Dromtrasna	49 B4	
Drum / *An Droim*	18 E5	
Co Monaghan / *Muineachán*		
Drum Co Roscommon	33 B3	
Drumahoe	3 B5	
Drumaness / *Droim an Easda*	20 E2	
Drumanure	40 H4	
Drumard	15 C3	
Drumatober	32 H5	
Drumbane / *An Drom Bán*	51 C1	
Drumbaun	42 H5	
Drumbeg	12 E5	
Drumbo	12 E5	
Drumcar / *Droim Chora*	28 E2	
Drumcharley	42 F3	
Drumcliff Co Clare	41 D3	
Drumcliff / *Droim Chliabh*	15 D2	
Co Sligo / *Sligeach*		
Drumcondra / *Droim Conrach*	27 C2	
Drumcree / Droim Cria	26 H5	
Drumfin / *Droim Fionn*	16 E5	
Drumfree / *Droim Fraoigh*	3 A3	
Drumgriftin	31 D3	
Druminnin	8 G3	
Drumkeary	42 G1	
Drumkeen	9 A1	
Drumkeeran / *Droim Caorthainn*	16 G4	
Drumlea / *Droim Léith*	25 D1	
Drumlish / *Droim Lis*	25 D3	
Drumlosh	33 C3	
Drummacool	16 F4	
Drummin / *An Dromainn*	40 F4	
Drummullin / *Droim Ailí*	25 B3	
Drumna	25 D1	
Drumnagreagh Port	6 F6	
Drumnakilly / *Droim na Coille*	10 E4	
Drumoghill	9 B1	
Drumone	26 H4	
Drumquin / *Droim Caoin*	9 C4	
Drumraney / *Droim Raithne*	33 D2	
Drumree / *Droim Rí*	35 D1	
Drumroe	61 C2	
Drumshanbo / *Droim Seanbhó*	16 G5	
Drumskinny / *Droim Scine*	9 A5	
Drumsna / *Droim ar Snámh*	25 B2	
Drumsurn / *Droim Sorn*	4 E5	
Drung	18 E5	
Duagh / *Dubháth*	49 A3	
Dually	51 D2	
Dublin / *Baile Átha Cliath*	36 F3	
Duggarry	33 B3	
Duleek / *Damhliag*	28 E5	
Dumfea	53 B1	
Dunadry / *Dún Eadradh*	11 D3	
Dunamon	24 H5	
Dunany / *Dún Áinne*	28 F2	
Dunbell	52 H1	
Dunboyne / *Dún Búinne*	36 E2	
Dunbyrne	35 B4	
Duncannon / *Dún Canann*	63 C3	
Duncormick / *Dún Chormaic*	64 E3	
Dundalk / *Dún Dealgan*	28 E1	
Dunderrow / *Dún Darú*	68 F1	
Dunderry	27 C5	
Dundian	18 F2	
Dundonald / *Dún Dónaill*	12 F4	
Dundoogan	32 H3	
Dundrod / *Dún dTrod*	11 D4	
Dundrum / *Dún Droma*	20 F3	
Co Down / *An Dún*		
Dundrum Co Dublin	36 F4	
Dundrum Co Tipperary	51 B2	
Dunfanaghy / *Dún Fionnachaidh*	2 F3	
Dungannon / *Dún Geanainn*	10 G5	
Dunganstown	53 A4	
Dungarvan / *Dún Garbháin*	53 A2	
Co Kilkenny / *Cill Chainnigh*		
Dungarvan / *Dún Garbhán*	62 E2	
Co Waterford / *Port Láirge*		
Dungiven / *Dún Geimhin*	10 F1	
Dunglow / *An Clochán Liath*	1 C5	
Dungourney / *Dún Guairne*	61 B4	
Dunhill	62 H1	
Duniry	42 H1	
Dunkerrin / *Dún Cairin*	43 C3	
Dunkineely / *Dún Cionnaola*	8 E4	
Dunkitt	52 H5	
Dunlavin / *Dún Luáim*	45 C1	
Dunleer / *Dún Léire*	28 E3	
Dunlewy / *Dún Lúiche*	2 E5	
Dunloy / *Dún Lathaí*	4 H5	
Dunmanus	66 G3	
Dunmanway / *Dún Mánmhaí*	67 C1	
Dunmoon	61 C3	
Dunmore / *Dún Mór*	24 F5	
Dunmore East / *Dún Mór*	63 B3	
Dunmurry / *Dún Muirigh*	11 D5	
Dunnamaggan / *Dún Iomagáin*	52 G3	
Dunnamanagh / *Dún na Manach*	9 D1	
Dunnamore / *Domhnach Mór*	10 F3	
Dunningstown	52 G1	
Dunquin / *Dún Chaoin*	57 B1	
Dunseverick / *Dún Sobhairce*	4 G2	
Dunshaughlin / *Dún Seachlainn*	35 D1	
Durrow / *Darú*	44 G4	
Durrus / *Dúras*	66 H2	
Dún Laoghaire	36 G4	
Dysart / *An Diseart*	34 F2	

E

Eadestown	35 D5	
Earlshill	52 E1	
Easky / *Iascaigh*	15 A3	
East Barrs	16 G3	
Eden / *An tEadan*	12 F3	
Edenderry / *Éadan Doire*	35 A3	

Ederney / Eadarnaidh 9 B5
Edgeworthstown / Meathas Troim 26 E4
Eglinton / An Mhagh 3 C4
Eglish / An Eaglais 18 G1
Eighter / Iochtar 26 H3
Ellistrin / Eileastran 2 G5
Elphin / Ail Finn 25 A3
Elton / Eiltiún 50 G3
Emlagh Cross Roads 32 F5
Emlaghmore 57 C4
Emly / Imleach 50 H3
Emmoo 25 B5
Emo / Ioma 44 H1
Emyvale / Scairbh an gCaorach 18 F2
Ennis / Inis 41 D4
Enniscorthy / Inis Córthaidh 53 D2
Enniskean / Inis Céin 67 D1
Enniskerry / Áth an Sceire 36 G5
Enniskillen / Inis Ceithleann 17 B2
Ennistimon / Inis Diomáin 40 G3
Erra 25 C4
Errill / Eiréil 44 E4
Esker / An Eiscir 32 F4
Esker South 25 D3
Esknaloughoge 58 E5
Eskragh / Eiscreach 18 E1
Eyeries / Ba hAorai 66 E1
Eyrecourt / Dún an Uchta 33 B5

F

Faha 58 G2
Fahaduff 49 A5
Fahamore 48 E5
Fahan / Fathain 3 A4
    Co Donegal / Dún na nGall
Fahanasoodry 50 H4
Fahy Co Galway 32 H4
Fahy Co Galway 33 A5
Fairfield 33 D2
Fairymount / Mullach na Sí 24 G3
Falcarragh / An Fál Carrach 2 E3
Fanore 40 G1
Farahy 60 G1
Fardrum / Fardroim 33 C3
Farmer's Bridge 48 G5
Farnagh 33 D3
Farnaght 25 D2
Farnanes / Na Fearnáin 67 B1
Farnoge 53 A4
Farran / An Fearann 60 E5
Farranfore / An Fearann Fuar 58 H1
Fauna 45 D2
Feakle / An Fhiacail 42 F3
Feaklecally 58 E3
Fedamore / Feadamair 50 F2
Feeard 48 F1
Feenagh Co Clare 40 G1
Feenagh / Fionach 50 E4
    Co Limerick / Luimneach
Feeny / Na Fineadha 10 F1
Fenagh / Fionnmhach 25 D1
Fenit / An Fhianait 48 F5
Fennagh / Fionnmhach 45 B5
Fennor / Fionnúir 62 H1
    Co Waterford / Port Láirge
Fennor Co Westmeath 34 H1
Feohanagh Co Kerry 57 B1
Feohanagh / An Fheothanach 49 D4

Co Limerick / Luimneach
Feoramore 58 G5
Ferbane / An Féar Bán 33 D4
Fermoy / Mainistir Fhear Maí 61 A2
Ferns / Fearna 54 E2
Ferry Bridge 50 E1
Ferrybank / Portan Chalaidh 46 G4
Fethard / Fiodh Ard 52 E3
    Co Tipperary / Tiobraid Árann
Fethard Co Wexford 63 C3
Fews 62 F1
Fiddane 42 H5
Fiddown / Fiodh Dúin 52 G4
Fieries 58 H1
Figlash 52 F4
Finavarra 31 C5
Finnea / Fiodh an Átha 26 G3
Finnis 19 D2
Finny / Fionnaithe 30 G1
Fintown / Baile na Finne 8 G1
Finuge / Fionnúig 48 H3
Finvoy / An Fhionnbhoith 4 G5
Firkeel 65 D2
Firmount 61 A3
Fisherstreet 40 F2
Five Corners 11 D2
Fiveally / An Chúirt 33 D5
Fivemilebourne / Abhainn an Chartúin 16 E3
Fivemilebridge 60 G5
Flagford 25 B2
Fivemiletown / Baile na Lorgan 17 D2
Flagmount / Leacain an Éadain 42 F2
    Co Clare / An Clár
Flagmount Co Kilkenny 53 A1
Flatfield 11 C5
Flemingstown 58 E1
Florence Court / Mullach na Seangán 17 A3
Flurrybridge 19 B5
Foilnamuck 66 H3
Fontstown 45 B1
Fordstown / Baile Forda 27 B5
Fore / Baile Fhobhair 26 H4
Forkill / Foirceal 19 B5
Formoyle Co Clare 40 G1
Formoyle Co Mayo 21 D4
Formoyle Co Longford 25 C5
Fornaght 60 F3
Fort Middle 50 E4
Fort William 43 B3
Forthill 33 C1
Foulkesmill / Muileann Fúca 53 C5
Foulkstown 51 D2
Four Mile House /
    Teach na gCeithre Mhile 25 A4
Four Roads / Tigh Srathra 33 A1
Fox Hill 22 G5
Foxfield / Cnocán an Mhada Rua 25 C1
Foxford / Béal Easa 23 C1
Foxhall 23 D5
Foynes / Faing 49 C1
Freemount / Cillin an Chrónáin 49 D5
Frenchpark / Dún Gar 24 H2
Freshford / Achadh Úr 44 G5
Freynestown 45 C2
Friarstown 50 F2
Frogmore 48 F5
Frosses / Na Frosa 8 F4
Fuerty 25 A5
Funshin More 41 D1
Furbogh 30 H4

Furraleigh 62 F1
Furroor 40 G5
Furrow 51 A5
Fybagh 58 F1

G

Gainstown 34 G2
Galbally / An Gallbhaile 50 H4
    Co Limerick / Luimneach
Galbally Co Wexford 53 D4
Galbertstown 51 D1
Galgorm / Galgorm 11 B1
Gallagh 25 B5
Galmoy / Gabhalmhaigh 44 E4
Galtrim 35 C1
Galway / Gaillimh 31 D4
Gannavane 51 A1
Garadice / Garairis 35 C2
Garbally 33 A3
Garlow Cross / Crois Chearla 27 D5
Garnavilla 51 C4
Garr 34 H3
Garrafrauns 24 E5
Garranard 14 G4
Garranereagh 59 D5
Garranlahan / An Garrán Leathan 24 F4
Garraun Co Clare 48 H1
Garraun Co Galway 32 H5
Garraun Co Kerry 58 G1
Garravoone 52 G5
Garrettstown 45 C3
Garrison / An Gasastún 16 G1
Garristown / Baile Gháire 36 E1
Garrycaheragh 61 A3
Garrycloonagh 14 G5
Garrycullen 53 C5
Garryduff 4 G4
Garryfine / Garrai Phaghain 50 F4
Garryhill 53 B1
Garrymore 61 B4
Garrynafana 43 B4
Garryspillane 50 H4
Garryvoe 61 B5
Garvagh / Garbhach 25 C1
    Co Leitrim / Liatroim
Garvagh / Garbhachadh 4 F5
    Co Londonderry / Doire
Garvaghy / Garbhachadh 10 E5
Gattabaun / An Geata Bán 44 F5
Gawleys Gate / Geata Mhic Amhlaí 11 B5
Gaybrook / Baile Réamainn 34 G2
Geashill / Géisill 34 G4
Geashill / An Ghaobhach 16 F5
Geevagh / An Ghaobhach 16 F5
Georgestown 62 G1
Gerahies 66 H2
Gibstown 27 C4
Gilford / Áth Mhic Giolla 19 B2
Glanalin 66 G3
Glandart 67 A2
Glandore / Cuan Dor 67 C3
Glangevlin 16 H4
Glanlough 66 G2
Glanmire / Gleann Maghair 60 H4
Glanoe 48 H4
Glanroon 66 F3
Glantane / An Gleanntán 60 E2
Glanworth / Gleannúir 60 H1

Glarryford / *An tÁth Glárach* — 4 H5
Glashabeg — 57 B1
Glashaboy East — 60 G3
Glashaboy North — 60 G3
Glashananoon — 49 A4
Glasleck / *Glasleic* — 27 B2
Glaslough / *Glasloch* — 18 G2
Glassan / *Glasán* — 33 C2
Glassillaun — 21 D2
Glastry — 12 H5
Glebe — 3 D3
Glen Of Imail / *Gleann Ó Máil* — 45 D2
Glen Of The Downs — 36 G5
Glen / *An Gleann* — 2 G3
  Co Donegal / *Dún na nGall*
Glen Co Londonderry — 10 H1
Glenacroghery — 61 B3
Glenade — 16 F2
Glenagort — 22 G1
Glenahilty — 43 B3
Glenard / *Gleann Aird* — 62 E3
Glenariff or Waterfoot / — 6 E4
  Gleann Aireamh
Glenarm / *Gleann Arma* — 6 F5
Glenavy / *Lann Abhaidh* — 11 C4
Glenbeigh — 58 E2
Glenboy / *Gleann Buí* — 16 G3
Glenbrien / *Gleann Bhriain* — 54 E3
Glenbrohane — 50 H4
Glencar — 58 F3
Glencoh — 30 F3
Glencolumbkille / *Gleann Cholm Cille* — 7 C3
Glencullen — 36 F4
Glendalough Co Waterford — 52 E5
Gleneely / *Gleann Daoile* — 3 C2
Glenfarne / *Gleann Fearna* — 16 H3
Glenflesk — 59 A3
Glengarriff / *An Gleann Garbh* — 66 H1
Glengoura — 61 B2
Glenhead — 3 D5
Glenlara — 13 B3
Glenmore Co Clare — 40 G5
Glenmore / *An Gleann Mhór* — 53 A4
  Co Kilkenny / *Cill Chainnigh*
Glennagat — 51 D4
Glennaknockane — 49 B5
Glennamaddy / *Gleann na Madadh* — 24 G5
Glennascaul — 31 D4
Glenoe — 12 F2
Glenough Lower — 51 B1
Glenough Upper — 51 B1
Glenroe — 50 H5
Glenshelane — 61 D1
Glentane Co Cork — 61 B3
Glentane Co Galway — 32 G2
Glenties / *Na Gleannta* — 8 F2
Glentogher / *Gleann Tóchair* — 3 B2
Glentrasna — 30 F2
Glenvale — 4 H5
Glenvar / *Gleann Bhairr* — 2 H3
Glenville / *Gleann an Phréacháin* — 60 H3
Glin / *An Gleann* — 49 B2
Glinsk Co Galway — 24 H5
Glinsk / *Glinsce (Connemara)* — 29 D3
Glounthaune — 60 H4
Glynn / *An Gleann* — 12 F2
  Co Antrim / *Aontroim*
Glynn Co Wexford — 53 B3
Glynn Co Wexford — 53 D4
Gneevgullia / *Gníomh go Leith* — 59 B2

Golden / *An Gabhailin* — 51 C3
Golden Ball — 36 G4
Goleen / *An Góilin* — 66 G4
Goold's Cross / *Crois an Ghúlaigh* — 51 C2
Goresbridge / *An Droichead Nua* — 53 A1
Gorey / *Guaire* — 54 F1
Gormanstown / *Baile Mhic Gormáin* — 28 F5
Gormanstown — 51 C5
Gort / *An Gort* — 42 E1
Gortaclady — 10 F4
Gortagowan — 58 F5
Gortahork / *Gort An Choirce* — 2 E3
Gortalough — 43 C5
Gortarevan — 33 B5
Gortaroo — 61 C4
Gorteen / *Goirtín* — 32 G3
  Co Galway / *Gaillimh*
Gorteen Co Kilkenny — 44 H4
Gorteen Co Limerick — 50 E4
Gorteen Co Sligo — 24 G1
Gorteen Co Waterford — 62 E3
Gorteens — 53 A5
Gorteeny / *Giortíní* — 42 H2
Gortgarriff — 66 E1
Gortgarrigan / *Gort Geargáin* — 16 F3
Gortglass — 59 A1
Gortin / *An Goirtín* — 9 D3
Gortleatilla — 14 E3
Gortletteragh — 25 D2
Gortmore Co Mayo — 14 G3
Gortnadeeve — 24 H5
Gortnahaha — 49 C1
Gortnahey — 3 D5
Gortnahoo / *Gort na hUamha* — 52 E1
Gortnahoughtee — 59 B5
Gortnahurra — 14 F4
Gortnaleaha — 48 G5
Gortnamearacaun — 42 E3
Gortnasillagh — 24 H3
Gortreagh / *An Gort Riabhach* — 10 G4
Gortrelig — 58 F3
Gortskeagh — 41 D1
Gowlaun — 21 D5
Gowlin — 53 B2
Gowran / *Gabhrán* — 53 A1
Gracehill / *Baile Uí Chinnéide* — 11 B1
Graiguearush — 62 F1
Graiguenamanagh / *Gráig na Manach* — 53 B2
Granabeg — 46 E1
Granagh — 50 E3
Granard / *Granard* — 26 F3
Graney — 45 B3
Grange / *Gráinseach Chuffe* — 52 G2
  Co Kilkenny / *Cill Chainigh*
Grange Co Kilkenny — 52 H5
Grange Co Offaly — 35 A3
Grange Co Tipperary — 51 D4
Grange / *An Ghráinseach* — 15 D2
  Co Sligo / *Sligeach*
Grange / *An Ghreainsigh* — 61 D3
  Co Waterford / *Port Láirge*
Grange Co Wexford — 64 E3
Grange Beg Co Kildare — 35 B5
Grange Beg Co Laois — 44 E3
Grange Con / *Gráinseach Choinn* — 45 C2
Grangebellew / *Greainseach an Dísirt* — 28 E3
Grangeford / *An Ghráinseach* — 45 C4
Grangegeeth — 27 D4
Grannagh — 32 E5
Grant House — 18 F1

Granville / *An Doire Mhin* — 10 G5
Greenan / *An Grainán* — 46 F3
Greenanstown / *Baile Uí Ghrianáin* — 28 F5
Greencastle / *An Caisleán Nua* — 3 D2
  Co Donegal / *Dún na nGall*
Greencastle / *Caisleán na hOireanaí* — 19 D5
  Co Down / *An Dún*
Greencastle Co Tyrone — 10 E3
Greenisland / *Inis Glas* — 12 E3
Greenland — 61 C4
Greenore / *Grianfort* — 19 D5
Grenagh / *Grenach* — 60 F3
Greyabbey / *An Mhainistir Liath* — 12 G5
Greygrove — 40 G5
Greysteel — 3 C4
Greystone / *An Chloch Liath* — 18 G1
Greystones / *Na Clocha Liatha* — 36 G5
Griston — 50 H4
Grogan — 33 D3
Groomsport / *Port an Ghialla Chruama* — 12 G3
Gubaveeny — 16 H3
Gulladuff — 10 H2
Gullaun — 59 B2
Gurteen / *Goirtín* — 16 F2
Gusserane / *Ráth na gCosarean* — 53 B5
Gweedore / *Gaoth Dobhair* — 1 D4
Gweesalia / *Gaoth Sáile* — 13 C5
Gyleen — 61 A5

H

Hackball's Cross — 27 D1
Hacketstown — 45 D3
Halfway House / *Tigh Leath Slí* — 63 B3
Hamiltonsbawn / *Bábhún Hamaltún* — 19 A2
Hannahstown / *Baile Haine* — 11 D4
Harristown — 52 H4
Hays — 27 D4
Headford / *Áth Cinn* — 31 C2
Headfort — 59 A3
Heathfield — 68 G1
Heavenstown — 53 D5
Heirhill — 48 F3
Helen's Bay / *Cuan Héilin* — 12 F3
Herbertstown / *Baile Hiobaird* — 50 G2
Highstreet — 33 C4
Hightown — 61 A3
Hill Of Down / *Cnoc an Dúin* — 35 A2
Hill Street — 25 B2
Hillhall — 11 D5
Hillsborough / *Cromghlinn* — 19 D1
Hilltown / *Baile Hill* — 19 D4
  Co Down / *An Dún*
Hilltown Co Wexford — 54 E5
Hilltown Co Wexford — 53 C5
Hollyford / *Áth an Chuilinn* — 51 B1
Hollyfort / *Ráth an Chuillinn* — 46 F5
Hollymount Co Galway — 42 F1
Hollymount / *Maolla* — 23 C5
  Co Mayo / *Maigh Eo*
Hollywood / *Cillín Chaoimhín* — 12 F4
Holycross / *Gaile na gCailleach* — 50 G3
  Co Limerick / *Luimneach*
Holycross / *Mainstir na Croiche* — 51 C1
  Co Tipperary / *Tiobraid Árann*
Holywell — 16 H3
Holywood / *Ard Mhic Nasca* — 12 F4
Horetown — 64 E3
Horse and Jockey / *An Marcach* — 51 D4

Horseleap / *Baile Átha an Urchair* — 34 E3
Hospital / *An tOspidéal* — 50 H3
Hough — 51 C1
Howth / *Binn Éadair* — 36 G3
Hugginstown — 52 H3
Hurlers Cross — 42 E5
Hyde Park — 11 D3

I

Illaunstookagh — 58 E2
Inagh / *Eigneagh* — 40 H3
Inch Co Kerry — 58 E1
Inch Co Tipperary — 51 B1
Inch / *An Inis*
 Co Wexford / *Loch Garman*
Inchabaun — 49 C4
Inchbeg — 44 G5
Inchigeelagh / *Inse Geimhleach* — 59 C5
Inchinapallas — 60 H1
Inchnamuck — 51 B5
Inishannon — 68 F1
Inishcrone / *Inis Caoin* — 14 H3
Inishrush — 11 A1
Iniskeen / *Inis Caoin* — 27 D1
Inistioge / *Inis Tióg* — 53 A3
Innfield / *An Bóthar Buí* — 35 B2
Inveran / *Indreabhan* — 30 G4
Irishtown / *An Baile Gaelach* — 24 E5
Irvinestown / *Baile an Irbhinigh* — 17 B1

J

Jamestown Co Laois — 44 H1
Jamestown Co Leitrim — 25 B2
Jenkinstown — 28 F1
Jenkinstown Co Kilkenny — 44 G5
Jerrettspass / *Bealach Sheirit* — 19 B3
Johnsfort — 23 D2
Johnstown / *Cill Sheanaigh* — 60 H5
 Co Cork / *Corcaigh*
Johnstown Co Kildare — 35 D4
Johnstown / *Baile Sheáin* — 44 F5
 Co Kilkenny / *Cill Chainnigh*
Johnstown Co Meath — 27 C5
Johnstown Co Wexford — 53 D5
Johnstown Co Wicklow — 46 G4
Johnstown Co Wicklow — 46 F4
Johnstown Bridge — 35 B3
Johnstownbridge — 25 C3
Johnswell / *Tobar Eoin* — 44 H5
Jonesborough / *Baile an Chláir* — 19 B5
Julianstown / *Baile Iuiliáin* — 28 F4

K

Kanturk / *Ceann Toirc* — 59 D1
Katesbridge / *Droichead Cháit* — 19 D2
Keadew / *Céideadh* — 16 G5
Keady / *An Céide* — 18 H3
Kealkill / *An Chaolchoill* — 67 A1
Kealvaugh — 59 B5
Keeagh — 30 H3
Keel / *An Caol* — 21 C1
Keelnagore — 57 D4
Keeloges — 24 G5
Keenagh / *Caonagh* — 25 D5
 Co Longford / *An Longfort*

Keenagh Co Mayo — 14 F5
Keereen — 61 D2
Kells Co Kerry — 57 D3
Kells Co Kilkenny — 52 G2
Kells Connor / *Na Cealla* — 11 C2
 Co Antrim / *Aontroim*
Kells/Ceananas — 27 B4
Kelshabeg — 45 D3
Kenmare / *Neidín* — 58 H4
Kentstown — 27 D5
Kerloge — 54 E5
Kesh / *An Cheis* — 9 A5
 Co Fermanagh / *Fear Manach*
Kesh Co Sligo — 16 E5
Keshcarrigan / *Ceis Charraigin* — 25 C1
Kilbaha / *Cill Bheathach* — 48 F2
Kilbane / *An Choill Bhán* — 42 G4
Kilbarry / *Cill Barra* — 52 H5
Kllilbeacanty — 42 E1
Kilbeg — 62 G1
Kilbeggan / *Cill Bheagáin* — 34 F3
Kilbegnet — 24 H5
Kilbeheny / *Coill Bheithne* — 51 A5
Kilberry / *Cill Bhearaigh* — 45 A2
 Co Kildare / *Cill Dara*
Kilberry Co Meath — 27 C4
Kilbrack — 52 F5
Kilbreedy Co Limerick — 50 F4
Kilbreedy Co Limerick — 50 E2
Kilbreedy Co Tipperary — 51 C2
Kilbrickan — 30 F3
Kilbrickane — 43 D5
Kilbricken / *Cill Bhriocáin* — 44 F2
Kilbride Co Mayo — 23 D2
Kilbride Co Meath — 27 B5
Kilbride / *Cill Bhride* — 46 G3
 Co Wicklow / *Cill Mhantáin*
Kilbride Co Wicklow — 36 E5
Kilbrien Co Cork — 60 H2
Kilbrien Co Waterford — 62 E1
Kilbrin — 60 E1
Kilbrittain / *Cill Briotáin* — 68 F2
Kilcaimin — 31 D4
Kilcappagh — 34 H5
Kilcar / *Cinn Charthaigh* — 7 D4
Kilcarney — 45 D3
Kilcarroll — 49 A1
Kilcash — 52 F4
Kilcashel — 33 B3
Kilcavan — 34 G5
Kilchreest / *Cill Chriost* — 32 F5
Kilclaran — 42 F3
Kilclief — 20 G2
Kilcloher — 48 F2
Kilclonfert — 34 G3
Kilcock / *Cill Choca* — 35 C3
Kilcoe — 67 A3
Kilcogy / *Cill Chóige* — 26 F3
Kilcohan — 63 B3
Kilcolgan / *Cill Cholgáin* — 32 E5
Kilcolman Co Cork — 68 E1
Kilcolman / *Cill Cholmain* — 49 C2
 Co Limerick / *Luimneach*
Kilcolman Co Waterford — 62 E3
Kilcomin — 43 C2
Kilcommon / *Cill Chuimín* — 51 C4
 Co Tipperary / *Tiobraid Árann*
Kilcommon Co Tipperary — 43 B5
Kilcon — 14 G4
Kilconierin — 32 F4

Kilconly / *Cill Chonla* — 31 D1
Kilconnell / *Cill Chonaill* — 32 H3
Kilconnor — 50 G5
Kilcoo / *Cill Chua* — 19 D3
Kilcoole / *Cill Chomhghaill* — 46 G1
Kilcor — 61 A2
Kilcorkan — 41 D2
Kilcormac (Frankford) / *Cill Chormaic* — 33 D5
Kilcornan — 50 E1
Kilcorney / *Cill Coirne* — 59 D2
Kilcotty / *Cill Chota* — 54 E3
Kilcredan — 61 C4
Kilcrohane / *Cill Chrócháin* — 66 G3
Kilcronat — 61 B3
Kilcullen / *Cill Chuillin* — 45 C1
Kilcummin Co Kerry — 58 H2
Kilcummin / *Cill Chuimín* — 47 D5
 Co Kerry / *Ciarraí*
Kilcurly / *Ciill Choirle* — 28 E1
Kilcurry / *Cill an Churraigh* — 19 B5
Kilcusnaun — 49 A5
Kildalkey / *Cill Dealga* — 35 B1
Kildangan / *Cill Daingin* — 45 A1
Kildanoge — 51 C5
Kildare / *Cill Dara* — 35 B5
Kildavin / *Cill Damhain* — 53 C1
Kildermody — 52 G5
Kildorrery / *Cill Dairbhre* — 50 H5
Kildress — 10 G4
Kilduffahoo — 50 H1
Kildurrihy — 57 B1
Kilfeakle — 51 B3
Kilfearagh — 48 G1
Kilfenora / *Cill Fhionnúrach* — 40 G2
Kilfinnane / *Cill Fhíonáin* — 50 G4
Kilfinny — 50 E2
Kilflynn / *Cill Flainn* — 48 G4
Kilgarvan / *Cill Gharbhain* — 59 A4
Kilglass Co Galway — 32 H2
Kilglass / *Cill Ghlais* — 33 B1
 Co Roscommon / *Ros Comáin*
Kilglass / Cill Ghlas — 15 A3
 Co Sligo / *Sligeach*
Kilgobnet / *Cill Ghobnait* — 58 G2
 Co Kerry / *Ciarraí*
Kilgowan — 45 C1
Kilgrogan — 50 E2
Kilkea — 45 B3
Kilkeasy — 52 H3
Kilkee / *Cill Chaoi* — 39 D5
Kilkeel / *Cill Chaoil* — 20 E5
Kilkelly / *Cill Cheallaigh* — 24 E2
Kilkenny / *Cill Chainnigh* — 52 G1
Kilkenny West — 33 D2
Kilkerran — 68 F2
Kilkerrin / *Cill Choirín* — 32 G1
Kilkieran / *Cill Chiaráin* — 30 E3
Kilkilleen — 67 A3
Kilkinlea — 49 B4
Kilkishen / *Cill Chisín* — 42 E4
Kill / *An Chill* — 26 H1
 Co Cavan / *An Cabhán*
Kill Co Kildare — 35 D4
Kill Co Waterford — 62 G1
Killachonna — 33 D2
Killaclug — 50 H5
Killacolla — 50 E4
Killadeas / *Cill Chéile Dé* — 17 B1
Killaderry — 32 H2
Killadoon / *Coill an Dúin* — 21 D4

Killadysert / *Cill an Disirt* — 49 C1
Killafeen — 42 E2
Killag — 64 E3
Killahaly — 61 C2
Killala / *Cill Ala* — 14 H3
Killallon — 27 A4
Killaloe — 42 G4
Killaloo — 10 E1
Killamery — 52 F3
Killane — 35 A3
Killateeaun — 22 G5
Killanena — 42 F2
Killann / *Cill Anna* — 53 C2
Killard — 40 E5
Killare — 34 E2
Killarga / *Cill Fhearga* — 16 F3
Killarney / *Cill Airne* — 58 H2
Killarone — 30 H2
Killaroo — 34 E2
Killashandra / *Cill na Seanrátha* — 26 F1
Killashee / *Cill na Sí* — 25 C4
Killasser / *Cill Lasrach* — 23 D1
Killaun — 43 D1
Killavally / *Coill an Bhaile* — 22 G4
Killavarilly — 61 A2
Killavarrig — 60 G3
Kiliavil / *Cill Fhábhail* — 15 D5
Killavoher — 32 F1
Killavullen / *Cill an Mhuilinnn* — 60 G2
Killea Co Donegal — 3 A5
Killea Co Leitrim — 16 G2
Killea / *Cill Shléibhe* — 43 C4
    Co Tipperary / *Tiobraid Árann*
Killea Co Waterford — 63 B3
Killead / *Cill Éad* — 11 C3
Killeagh / *Cill Ia* — 61 C4
Killeany — 39 D1
Killedmond — 53 B1
Killeedy — 49 C4
Killeen Co Galway — 42 E2
Killeen Co Mayo — 21 D4
Killeen Co Tipperary — 43 C1
Killeen Co Tyrone — 10 H5
Killeenaran — 31 D5
Killeenasteena — 51 C3
Killeenavarra — 32 E5
Killeeneenmore — 32 E5
Killeenleagh — 67 A2
Killeens Cross — 60 G4
Killerrig — 45 C4
Killeevan — 18 E4
Killeglan — 33 A2
Killeigh / *Cill Aichidh* — 34 F5
Killemadeema — 32 G5
Killen / *Cillin* — 9 B3
Killenagh — 54 F1
Killenaule / *Cill Náile* — 43 C1
    Co Tipperary / *Tiobraid Árann*
Killenaule Co Tipperary — 52 E2
Killeshil — 34 G3
Killeter / *Coill Íochtair* — 9 B4
Killimer — 49 A1
Killimor / *Cill Íomair* — 33 A5
Killinaboy / *Cill Inine Baoith* — 40 H2
Killinardrish / *Cill an Ard-dorais* — 60 E4
Killinaspick — 52 H4
Killinchy / *Cill Dhuinsí* — 12 G5
Killincooly — 54 F3
Killiney / *Cill Iníon Léinin* — 36 G4
    Co Dublin / *Baile Átha Cliath*

Killiney Co Kerry — 48 E5
Killinick / *Cill Fhionnóg* — 54 E5
Killinierin / *Cill an Iarainn* — 46 F5
Killinkere / *Cillin Chéir* — 27 A2
Killinny — 41 D1
Killinthomas — 35 A4
Killiskey — 46 G1
Killmacahill — 61 B5
Killogeary — 14 G3
Killogeenaghan — 33 D3
Killaghteen — 49 C3
Killoe — 26 E4
Killoluaig — 57 C4
Killomoran — 42 E1
Killoneen — 34 G4
Killoran / *Cill Odhráin* — 32 H4
Killorglin / *Cill Orglan* — 58 F2
Killoscobe — 32 G2
Killough / *Cill Locha* — 20 G3
Killour — 22 H5
Killsallaghan — 36 F2
Killucan / *Cill Liúcainne* — 34 H1
Killukin — 25 B2
Killurin (Offaly) — 34 E5
KIllurin (Wexford) / *Cill Liúráin* — 53 D4
Killurly — 57 C5
Killusty — 52 E3
Killybegs Co Antrim — 11 B2
Killybegs / *Na Cealla Beaga* — 8 E4
    Co Donegal / *Dún na nGall*
Killyclogher — 9 D4
Killygar — 26 E1
Killygordon / *Cúil na gCuiridín* — 9 B2
Killykergan / *Coill Uí Chiaragain* — 4 F5
Killylea / *Coillidh Léith* — 18 G2
Killyleagh / *Cill Ó Laoch* — 20 G1
Killyneill / *Coill Uí Néill* — 18 G3
Killyon — 43 D1
Kilmacanoge / *Cill Mocheanóg* — 36 G5
Kilmacow / *Cill Mhic Bhúith* — 52 H5
Kilmacrenan / *Cill Mhic Réanáin* — 2 G4
Kilmacthomas / *Coill Mhic Thomáisín* — 62 F1
Kilmactranny / *Cill Mhic Treana* — 16 F5
Kilmaganny / *Cill Mogeanna* — 52 G3
Kilmaine / *Cill Mheáin* — 31 C1
Kilmainham Wood / *Cill Maighneann* — 27 B3
Kilmalady — 34 E3
Kilmaley / *Cill Mháille* — 40 H4
Kilmalin — 36 G5
Kilmallock / *Cill Mocheallóg* — 50 G4
Kilmanagh / *Cill Mhanach* — 52 F1
Kilmaniheen — 49 A4
Kilmeadan / *Cill Mhíodháin* — 52 H5
Kilmeage / *Cill Maodhog* — 35 B4
Kilmeedy / *Cill Mide* — 49 D4
Kilmessan / *Cill Mheasáin* — 35 C1
Kilmicheal / *Cill Mhichil* — 59 C5
Kilmihil / *Cill Mhichil* — 40 G5
Kilmona — 60 G3
Kilmoon — 67 A4
Kilmore / *An Chill Mhór* — 19 A1
    Co Armagh / *Ard Mhaca*
Kilmore Co Cavan — 26 F1
Kilmore Co Clare — 42 F5
Kilmore Co Down — 20 F1
Kilmore Co Mayo — 23 C1
Kilmore / *Cill Mhór* — 25 B2
    Co Roscommon / *Ros Comáin*
Kilmore / *An Chill Mhór* — 64 E3
    Co Wexford / *Loch Garman*

Kilmore Quay / *Cé na Cille Móire* — 64 E3
Kilmore Upper — 25 C4
Kilmorna / *Cill Mhaonaigh* — 49 A3
Kilmorony — 45 A3
Kilmovee — 24 F2
Kilmuckridge / *Cill Mhucraise* — 54 F2
Kilmurry Co Clare — 42 E4
Kilmurry / *Cill Mhuire* — 40 F4
    Co Clare / *An Clár*
Kilmurry / *Cill Mhuire* — 59 D5
    Co Cork / *Corcaigh*
Kilmurry Co Limerick — 50 E4
Kilmurry Co Limerick — 50 H2
Kilmurry Co Wicklow — 45 C3
Kilmurry McMahon / — 49 B1
    Cill Mhuire Mhic Mhathúna
Kilmurvy / *Cill Mhuirbhigh* — 30 E5
Kilmyshall — 53 D1
Kilnacreagh — 42 F5
Kilnagross / *Coill na gCros* — 25 C1
Kilnahown — 32 H4
Kilnaleck / *Cill na Leice* — 26 G2
Kilnamanagh / *Cill na Manach* — 54 F2
Kilnamartery — 59 C4
Kilnamona / *Cill na Móna* — 40 H3
Kilpatrick — 68 F1
Kilpedder — 46 G1
Kilquane — 57 B1
Kilquiggin — 45 D4
Kilraghts / *Cill Reachtais* — 4 H4
Kilrane / *Cill Ruáin* — 54 F5
Kilrea / *Cill Ria* — 4 G5
Kilrean / *Cill Riáin* — 8 E2
Kilreekill / *Cill Rícill* — 32 H4
Kilroghter — 31 C3
Kilronan / *Cill Rónáin* — 39 D1
Kilroosky — 25 B5
Kilross / *Cill Ros* — 51 H3
Kilrush / *Cill Rois* — 48 H1
Kilsallagh / *Coill Salach* — 24 G5
    Co Galway / *Gaillimh*
Kilsallagh / *Coil Salach* — 22 E3
    Co Mayo / *Maigh Eo*
Kilsaran — 28 E2
Kilshanchoe — 35 B3
Kilshannig — 48 E5
Kilshanny / *Cill Seanaigh* — 40 G2
Kilsheelan — 52 E4
Kilshinahan — 68 E2
Kilskeer / *Cill Scire* — 27 A4
Kilskeery / *Cill Scire* — 17 B1
Kiltamagh — 23 D3
Kiltarsaghaun — 22 G4
Kiltartan — 42 E1
Kiltealy / *Cill Téile* — 53 C2
Kilteel — 35 D4
Kilteely / *Cill Tíle* — 50 H2
Kilteevan — 25 B5
Kiltegan — 45 D3
Kiltiernan / *Cill Tiarnáin* — 36 G4
    Co Dublin / *Baile Átha Cliath*
Kiltiernan Co Galway — 32 E5
Kiltober — 34 F3
Kiltoom / *Cill Tuama* — 33 B2
    Co Roscommon / *Ros Camáin*
Kiltoom Co Westmeath — 26 G5
Kiltormer / *Cill Tormóir* — 33 A4
Kiltullagh / *Cill Tulach* — 32 F4
Kiltyclogher / *Coilte Clochair* — 16 G2
Kilvemnon — 52 F3

Kilvine 24 E5
Kilwaughter / Cill Uachtair 12 E1
Kilwoghan 35 D3
Kilworth / Cill Uird 61 A1
Kilworth Camp 61 A1
Kinard 49 B2
Kinawley / Cill Náile 17 B3
Kingarrow 8 G1
Kingscourt / Dún an Rí 27 B2
Kingsland 24 H2
Kingsmill 10 H4
Kinlough / Cionn Locha 16 F1
Kinnegad / Cionn Átha Gad 34 H2
Kinnitty / Cionn Eitigh 43 D1
Kinsale / Cionn tSáile 68 G1
Kinsalebeg / Baile an Phoill 61 D3
Kinsaley 36 G2
Kinvarra Co Galway 30 F3
Kinvarra / Cinn Mhara 31 D5
    Co Galway / Gaillimh
Kircubbin / Cill Ghobáin 12 G5
Kirkhills 4 G4
Kirkistown 20 H1
Kishkeam / Coiscím na Caillí 59 C1
Knights Town 57 C4
Knock / An Cnoc 49 A1
    Co Clare / An Clár
Knock Co Mayo 23 D3
Knock Co Tipperary 44 E3
Knockacaurhin 40 H3
Knockaderry / Cnoc an Doire 49 D3
Knockagurraun 30 H4
Knockainy / Cnoc Áine 50 G3
Knockalafalla 52 F5
Knockalaghta 24 H4
Knockalough /Cnoc an Eanaigh 40 G5
Knockalunkard 40 H3
Knockananna / Cnoc an Eanaigh 46 E3
Knockanarra 24 E4
Knockane 59 D5
Knockanevin / Cnocán Aobhainn 50 H5
Knockanore 61 C3
Knockanure 49 A3
Knockaroe 44 E3
Knockaun 32 H5
Knockaunarast 61 C1
Knockaunbrack 49 A4
Knockaunnaglashy 58 F2
Knockaunroe 58 E2
Knockayrogeen 57 C1
Knockboy / An Cnoc Buí 62 E1
Knockbrack Co Clare 42 F4
Knockbrack / An Cno Breac 9 B1
    Co Donegal / Dún na nGall
Knockbrack Co Kerry 48 G4
Knockbride 27 A1
Knockbridge / Droichead an Cnoic 27 D1
Knockbrit / Cnoc an Bhriotaigh 51 D3
Knockbrown 68 E2
Knockburden 60 F5
Knockcloghrim / Cnoc Clochdhroma 10 H2
Knockcroghery / Cnoc an Chrochaire 33 B1
Knockdarnan 50 F3
Knockdrin 34 G1
Knockdrislagh 60 F2
Knockeenadallane 59 B1
Knockeencreen 49 A5
Knocklofty 51 D4
Knocklong / Cnoc Loinge 50 H3
Knockmael 42 E2

Knockmore / An Cnoc Mór 23 C1
Knockmourne 61 B2
Knocknaboley 40 G4
Knocknacurra 68 F1
Knocknagashel / Cnoc na gCaiseal 49 A4
Knocknageeha 66 H3
Knocknagower 42 G3
Knocknagree 59 B2
Knocknahaha 48 G5
Knocknahila 40 F4
Knocknahilan 60 E5
Knocknalina 13 C3
Knocknalower 13 D3
Knocknaskagh 61 B4
Knockraha / Cnoc Rátha 60 H4
Knockroe Co Cork 67 A3
Knockroe Co Kerry 58 E4
Knockroe Co Waterford 62 E2
Knocks Co Cork 67 D2
Knocks Co Laois 44 F2
Knockskagh 67 D2
Knockskavane 49 D5
Knocktopher / Cnoc an Tóchair 52 H3
Knockvicar 25 A1
Knuttery 60 G2
Kyle 44 H2
Kyleballyhue 45 B4
Kylebrack / An Choill Bhreac 32 G5
Kylegarve 51 A1

L

Labasheeda / Leaba Shíoda 49 B1
Laban 32 E5
Lack / An Leac 9 B5
Lackagh 35 A5
Lackamore / An Leac Mhór 42 H4
Lackan Cross 33 A1
Lackan Co Carlow 45 A5
Lackan Co Roscommon 25 B4
Lackan Co Westmeath 26 F5
Lackan / An Leacain 36 E5
    Co Wicklow / Cill Mhantáin
Lackareagh 59 D5
Lackbrooder 49 A5
Lacken / Leacain 53 B4
Lacken Co Kilkenny 52 G1
Lackendarragh North 60 H2
Lackey 44 E2
Ladysbridge / Droichead na Scuab 61 B4
Lagavara 4 H2
Lagganstown 51 C3
Laghey Corner 10 H5
Laghy / An Lathaigh 8 G4
Lahardaun 22 H1
Lakyle 49 B1
Lambeg / Lann Bheag 11 D5
Lamoge 52 G3
Lanesborough / Béal Átha Liag 25 C5
Lannaght 42 F2
Laracor 35 C1
Laragh Co Kildare 35 C3
Laragh Co Wicklow 46 F2
Largan Co Mayo 14 E4
Largan Co Roscommon 25 B3
Largan Co Sligo 15 A5
Largy 7 D4
Largydonnell 16 E1
Larne / Latharna 12 F1

Latnamard 18 F4
Lattin / Laitean 51 A3
Latton 18 F5
Lauragh 66 F1
Laurelvale / Tamhnaigh Bhealtaine 19 B2
Laurencetown / An Baile Mór 33 A4
Lavagh / Leamhach 15 C5
Lawrencetown / Baile Labhráis 19 B2
Lady's Island 64 G3
Laytown / An Inse 28 F4
Leamlara / Léim Lára 61 A4
Leap / An Léim 67 C3
Lecarrow / An Leithcheathrú 33 B1
Leckemy / Leic Éime 3 C2
Leenaun / An Líonán 22 E5
Legan or Lenamore 26 E5
Leggah 26 E2
Legoniel / Lag an Aoil 11 D4
Lehinch / An Leacht 40 F4
Leighlinbridge / Leithghlinn an Droichid 45 A5
Leitrim Co Clare 40 F5
Leitrim Co Down 20 E3
Leitrim Co Leitrim 25 B1
Leitrim East 49 A2
Leixlip / Lím an Bhradáin 36 E3
Lemanaghan 33 D4
Lemybrien / Léim Uí Bhriain 62 F1
Leperstown 63 B3
Lerrig 48 G4
Letterbreen / Leitir Bhruín 17 A2
Letterfrack / Leitir Fraic 29 D1
Letterkelly 40 G4
Letterkenny / Leitir Ceanainn 2 G5
Letterloan 4 F4
Lettermacaward / Leitir Mhic an Bhaird 8 E1
Lettermullan / Leitir Mealláin 30 E4
Lettermore 30 E4
Levally / An Leathbhaile 32 F1
    Co Galway / Gaillimh
Levally Co Mayo 23 C5
Licketstown 52 H5
Lifford 9 C2
Limavady / Léim an Mhadaidh 3 D4
Limerick / Luimneach 50 F1
Limerick Junction / Gabhal Luimnigh 51 A3
Lisbellaw / Líos Béal Átha 17 C2
Lisburn / Lios na gCearrbhach 11 D5
Liscananaun 31 D3
Liscannor / Lios Ceannúir 40 F3
Liscarney / Lios Cearnaigh 22 F4
Liscarroll / Lios Cearúill 50 E5
Liscloon / Lios Claon 9 D1
Liscrona 48 G1
Lisdargan 57 D1
Lisdoonvarna / Lios Dúin Bhearna 40 G2
Lisdowney 44 G4
Lisduff / An Lios Dubh 27 A3
    Co Cavan / An Cabhán
Lisduff Co Cork 60 G3
Lisduff Co Offaly 33 D5
Lisgarode 43 B3
Lisgoold 61 A3
Lisheen 41 D5
Lisheenaguile 33 A5
Liskeagh 24 H1
Lismaccfry 26 F4
Lismire 59 D1
Lismore / Lios Mór 61 C2
Lismoyle 33 B1
Lisnadill / Lios na Daille 18 H3
Lisnageer / Lios na gCaor 18 E5

Lisnagry / *Lios na Graí* 50 G1
Lisnakill Cross 62 H1
Lisnamuck / *Lios na Muc* 10 H2
Lisnarrick / *Lios na nDaróg* 17 A1
Lisnaskea / *Lios na Scéithe* 17 C3
Lispatrick 68 G2
Lispole / *Lios Póil* 57 D1
Lisroe 40 H4
Lisronagh / *Lios Ruanach* 52 E4
Lisryan 26 F4
Lissacresig 59 C4
Lissaha 51 D2
Lissalway / *Lios Sealbhaigh* 24 H4
Lissamona 66 H4
Lissanacody 33 A5
Lissananny 24 G3
Lissavard 67 D3
Lisselton / *Lios Eiltin* 48 H3
Lissycasey / *Lios Uí Chathasaigh* 40 H5
Listellick 48 G5
Listerlin 53 A4
Listooder 20 F1
Listowel / *Lios Tuathail* 48 H3
Lisvarrinane / *Lios Fearnáin* 51 A4
Littleton / *An Baile Beag* 51 D1
Lixnaw / *Leic Snámha* 48 G4
Loanends / *Carn Mhéabha* 11 D3
Lobinstown / *Baile Lóibín* 27 C3
Loch Gowna 26 F2
Loghill / *Leamhchoill* 49 B2
  Co Limerick / *Luimneach*
Loghill / *Co Limerick* 49 D3
Logleagh 61 B1
Lombardstown / *Baile Limbaird* 60 E2
Londonderry / *Doire* 3 B5
Longford / *An Longfort* 25 D4
  Co Longford / *An Longfort*
Longford Co Offaly 43 D1
Longwood / *Maigh Dearmahaí* 35 B2
Lorrha / *Lothra* 43 B1
Lorum 53 B1
Loskeran 62 E3
Loughaclerybeg 32 G3
Loughacutteen 51 C4
Loughanaboll 15 B4
Loughanavally 34 F2
Loughanbeg 30 G4
Loughanure 1 D1
Loughbrickland / *Loch Bricleann* 19 C2
Loughduff 26 F2
Lougher 58 E1
Loughgall / *Loch gCál* 19 A1
Loughglinn / *Loch Glinne* 24 G3
Loughguile / *Loch gCaol* 4 H4
Loughinisland / *Loch an Oileánn* 20 F2
Loughmoe / *Luachma* 43 D5
Loughmorne / *Loch Morn* 18 G5
Loughrea / *Baile Loch Riach* 32 G5
Loughshinny 36 G1
Louisburgh / *Cluain Cearbán* 22 E3
Louth / *Lú* 27 D1
Lowertown 66 G3
Lowtown 19 D2
Lucan / *Leamhcán* 36 E3
Lugdoon 15 B3
Luggacurren / *Log an Churraigh* 44 H3
Lukeswell 52 H4
Lullymore 35 B4
Lurgan / *An Lorgain* 19 B1
  Co Armagh / *Ard Mhaca*

Lurgan Co Roscommon 24 H2
Lurganboy Co Donegal 2 H3
Lurganboy Co Leitrim 16 F2
Lusk / *Lusca* 36 G1
Lyracrumpane / *Ladhar an Chrompáin* 48 H4
Lyradane 60 F3
Lyre /
Ladhar an Chrompáin or An Ladhar 60 E2
  Co Cork / *Corcaigh*
Lyre Co Kerry 49 A5
Lyre Co Waterford 61 B3
Lyrenaglogh 61 B1

M

Maam Cross 30 F2
Maas 8 E2
Mace 22 G3
Mackan / *Macan* 17 B3
Macosquin / *Maigh Choscáin* 4 F4
Macroney 61 A1
Macroom / *Maigh Chromtha* 59 D4
Madabawn 27 A1
Maddockstown / *Baile Mhadóg* 52 H1
Maganey / *Maigh Geine* 45 B3
Maghaberry 11 C5
Maghera Co Down 20 E3
Maghera / *Machaire Rátha* 10 H1
  Co Londonderry / *Doire*
Maghera Cross 42 E3
Magherafelt / *Machaire Fíolta* 10 H2
Magheralin / *Machaire Lainne* 19 C1
Magheramason 3 B5
Magheramorne / *Machaire Morna* 12 F2
Magheraveely / *Machaire Mhílie* 17 D4
Maghery / *An Machaire* 8 E1
  Co Donegal / *Dún na nGall*
Maghery Co Armagh 11 A5
Magilligan / *Aird Mhic Giollagain* 3 D3
Maguiresbridge / *Droichead Mhig Uidir* 17 B3
Mahoonagh 49 D3
Mainham 35 C3
Malahide / *Mullach Íde* 36 G2
Malin / *Málainn* 3 B1
Malin Beg / *Málainn Bhig* 7 B3
Malin More 7 B3
Mallaranny / *An Mhala Raiothní* 22 E2
Mallow / *Mala* 60 F2
Mallusk / *Maigh Bhloisce* 11 D3
Manorcunninngham / 2 H5
  Mainéar Uí Chuinneagáin
Manorhamilton / *Cluainín* 16 F3
Manselstown 43 D5
Mansfieldstown 28 E2
Mantua / *An Mointeach* 25 A3
Manulla 23 C3
Marble Arch 17 A3
Mardyke 52 E2
Margymonaghan 3 D3
Markethill / *Cnoc an Mhargaidh* 19 A3
Markhamstown 51 D4
Marlfield 51 D4
Marshalstown / *Baile Mharascail* 53 D2
Martinstown / *Baile Uí Mháirtín* 5 D5
Martinstown Co Limerick 50 G4
Marty 27 B4
Mastergeehy 57 D4
Masterstown 51 C3
Matehy 60 F4

Maulatrahane 67 B3
Maulavanig 67 A1
Maulawaddra 66 G3
Maum / *An Mám* 30 F1
Mauricesmills / *Muilte Mhuiris* 40 H3
Mayglass 54 E5
Maynooth / *Maigh Naud* 35 D3
Mayo / *Maigh Eo* 23 C4
Mayobridge / *Droichead Mhaigh Eo* 19 C4
Mazetown 11 D5
McGregor's Corner 5 D5
McLaughlins Corner 4 G5
Meanus / *Méanos* 50 F2
Meelick 33 B5
Meelin / *An Mhaoilinn* 49 C5
Meenaclady 1 D3
Meenacross 8 E1
Meenaneary 7 D3
Meenbannad 1 C1
Meenbannivane 49 A5
Meenglass 9 A2
Meennaraheeny 49 B5
Meigh 19 B4
Menlough Co Galway 32 G2
Menlough / *Mionlach* 31 C4
  Co Galway / *Gaillimh*
Middlequarter 61 D1
Middletown / *Coillidh Chanannain* 18 G3
Midfield / *An Trian Láir* 23 D2
Midleton / *Mainistir na Corann* 61 A4
Milehouse / *Teach an Mhíle* 53 D2
Milemill 45 C1
Milestone / *Cloch an Mhile* 51 B1
Milford / *Áth an Mhuilinn* 18 H2
  Co Armagh / *Ard Mhacha*
Milford / *Átha an Mhuilinn* 50 E4
  Co Cork / *Corcaigh*
Mill Brook 17 D4
Mill Town / *Baile an Mhuilinn* 11 C3
Millbrook / *Sruthán an Mhuilinnn* 12 E1
Millford / *Baile na nGallóglach* 2 G4
Millisle / *Oilean an Mhuilinn* 12 H4
Millstreet / *Sráid an Mhuilinn* 61 A1
  Co Cork / *Corcaigh*
Millstreet Co Cork 59 C2
Millstreet Co Waterford 61 D1
Milltown Co Armagh 19 A2
Milltown / *Baile an Mhuilinn* 17 C5
  Co Cavan / *An Cabhán*
Milltown Co Donegal 8 F4
Milltown Co Donegal 2 G3
Milltown Co Dublin 36 E3
Milltown Co Galway 32 G1
Milltown Co Galway 24 E5
Milltown Co Kerry 57 C1
Milltown Co Kerry 58 G1
Milltown Co Kildare 35 B5
Milltown Co Kilkenny 52 H4
Milltown Co Londonderry 4 E3
Milltown Co Londonderry 4 F4
Milltown Co Tyrone 10 E4
Milltown Co Westmeath 34 F1
Milltown Malbay / *Sráid na Cathrach* 40 F4
Milltownpass / 34 H2
  Belach Bhaile an Mhuilinn
Minane Bridge / 68 H1
  Droichead an Mhionnáin
Minerstown / *Baile na Mianadóirí* 20 F3
Minorstown 52 E4
Mitchelstown / *Baile Mhistéala* 51 A5

Moanmore Co Clare 48 H1
Moanmore Co Tipperary 50 H3
Moat Farrell 26 E4
Moate / *An Móta* 33 D3
Model Village (Cork) 60 F4
Model Village (Cork) 60 E4
Modelligo 61 D2
Modreeny 43 B3
Mogeely / *Maigh Dhíle* 61 B4
Mohil 44 H5
Mohill / *Maothail* 25 C2
Moira / *Maigh Rath* 11 C5
Moll's Gap 58 G4
Monagear 54 E2
Monaghan / *Muineachán* 18 F3
Monagoun 61 B2
Monaincha Bog 43 D3
Monalour 61 C1
Monamolin / *Muine Moling* 54 F2
Monamraher 62 E3
Monard Co Tipperary 51 A3
Monard Co Waterford 61 C1
Monaseed / *Móin na Saighead* 46 E5
Monaster / *An Mhainistir* 50 F2
Monasteraden / *Mainistir Réadáin* 24 G2
Monasterevin / *Mainistir Eimhín* 35 A5
Monea / *Maigh Niadh* 17 A2
Moneen Co Clare 48 F2
Moneen Co Galway 31 D2
Monettibog 34 F5
Moneycusker 59 C5
Moneydig / *Muine Dige* 4 F5
Moneygall / *Muine Gall* 43 C3
Moneyglass / *An Muine Glas* 11 B2
Moneymore Co Donegal 2 E5
Moneymore / *Muine Mór* 10 H3
Moneyneany / *Món na nIonadh* 10 G2
Moneyslane 19 D3
Moneyreagh / *Monadh Riabhach* 12 F5
Monilea / *An Muine Liath* 34 G1
Monivea / *Muine Mhéa* 32 F3
Monkstown / *Baile na Manach* 12 E3
   Co Antrim / *Aontroim*
Monkstown / *Baile na Mhanach* 60 H5
   Co Cork / *Corcaigh*
Montpelier 42 G5
Mooncoin / *Móin Choinn* 52 H5
Moone / *Maoin* 45 B2
Montpelier 42 G5
Moord 61 D4
Moorfields / *Péairc an tSléibhe* 11 C2
Morenane 50 E3
Mornington / *Baile Uí Mhornáin* 28 F4
Moroe / *Maigh Rua* 50 H1
Mortlestown 50 G4
Moskeagh 60 E5
Mosney Camp 28 F5
Moss-side / *Mas Saide* 4 H3
Mossley / *Maslaí* 12 E3
Mothel 52 F5
Mountbellew / *An Creagán* 32 G2
Mount Nugent / *Droichead Uí Dhálaigh* 26 G3
Mount Stewart 12 G5
Mount Talbot / *Mun Talbóid* 33 A1
Mount Temple / *An Grianan* 33 D2
   Co Westmeath
Mount Temple Co Sligo 15 D1
Mount Uniacke / *Cúil O gCorra* 61 B3
Mountallen 16 G5
Mountbolus / *Cnocán Bhólais* 34 E5
Mountcatherine 60 H3

Mountcharles / *Moin Searlas* 8 F4
Mountcollins / *Cnoc Uí Choileáin* 49 B5
Mountfield / *Achadh Ard* 10 E4
Mountjoy / *Muinseo* 9 D4
Mountmellick / *Moointeach Milie* 44 G1
Mountnorris / *Achadh na Cranncha* 19 A3
Mountrath / *Maiglean Rátha* 44 F2
Mountshannon / *Baile Uí Bhealáin* 42 H3
Moveen 48 G1
Moville / *Bun an Phobail* 3 D3
Moy Co Galway 41 D1
Moy / *An Maigh* 18 H1
   Co Tyrone / *Tir Eoghain*
Moyard / *Maigh Ard* 29 C1
Moyasta / *Maigh Sheasta* 48 H1
Moycarky 51 D1
Moycullen / *Maigh Cuilinn* 31 C3
Moydow / *Maigh Dumha* 25 D5
Moygashel / *Maigh gCaisil* 10 H5
Moyglass / *Maigh Ghlas* 51 D2
Moyle 45 B4
Moylisha 45 D5
Moylough / *Maigh Locha* 32 G2
   Co Galway / *Gaillimh*
Moylough Co Sligo 24 F1
Moymore 42 E4
Moynalty / *Maigh Locha* 27 B3
Moynalvy 35 C2
Moyne Co Wicklow 46 E3
Moyne Co Longford 26 E2
Moyne / *An Mhaighean* 24 G3
   Co Roscommon / *Ros Comáin*
Moyne Co Tipperary 43 D5
Moyrahan 13 C3
Moyreen 49 B2
Moyrus 29 D3
Moys 3 D5
Moyvally / *Maigh Bhealaigh* 35 B2
Moyvane (Newtown Sandes) / 49 A3
   Maigh Mheain
Moyvore / *Maigh Mhórdha* 34 E1
Moyvoughly / *Maig Bhachla* 33 D2
Mt. Melleray Monastery 61 C1
Muckamore / *Maigh Chomair* 11 C3
Mucklon 35 B3
Muckross 58 H3
Muckrush 31 C3
Muff / *Magh* 3 B4
Muinganear 49 A5
Muingaphuca 58 F2
Muingwee 49 A4
Muingydowda 57 C4
Mulhuddart / *Mullach Eadrad* 36 E3
Mullafarry 14 G4
Mullagh / *An Mullach* 27 A3
   Co Cavan / *An Cabhán*
Mullagh / *Mullach* 40 F4
   Co Clare / *An Clár*
Mullagh Co Galway 32 H5
Mullagh Co Mayo 22 E4
Mullagh Co Meath 35 D2
Mullaghbane 19 A5
Mullaghmacormick 25 C3
Mullaghmore / *An Mullach Mór* 16 E1
Mullaghroe 24 G1
Mullan Head 4 G5
Mullan Co Londonderry 4 F4
Mullan / *An Muileann* 18 G2
   Co Monaghan / *Muineachán*
Mullany's Cross 15 B5
Mullen 24 H3

Mullenaboree 60 G2
Mullennaglogh 52 F3
Mullennakill 53 A3
Mullinacuff / *Muileann Mhic Dhuibh* 45 D4
Mullinahone / *Muileann na hUamhan* 52 F2
Mullinavat / *Muileann an Bhata* 52 H4
Mullingar / *An Muileann gCear* 34 G1
Multyfarnham / *Muilte Farannáin* 26 G5
Mungret / *Mungairit* 50 F1
Murher 49 A3
Murntown / *Baile Mhúráin* 54 E5
Murreagh / *An Mhulríoch* 57 B1
Murrisk / *Muraisc* 22 F3
Murroogh 40 G1
Mweennalaa 48 H5
Myross 67 C3
Myshall / *Miseal* 45 C5

N

Naas / *An Nás* 35 C5
Nad 60 E2
Nahana 34 H5
Naran 8 E2
Narraghmore / *An Fhorrach Mhór* 45 B1
Naul / *An Aill* 28 F5
Navan / *An Uaimh* 27 C5
Neale / *An Éill* 30 H1
Nealstown 44 E2
Nedanone 58 E5
Nenagh / *An tAonach* 43 A4
New Birmingham / *Gleann an Ghuail* 52 E1
New Buildings / *An Baile Nua* 3 B5
New Chapel Cross 57 D5
New Inn / *An Dromainn* 26 H2
   Co Cavan / *An Cabhán*
New Inn / *An Cnoc Breac* 32 G4
   Co Galway / *Gailllimh*
New Inn Co Laois 44 H1
New Kildimo 50 E1
New Ross / *Ros Mhic Thriúin* 53 B4
New Twopothouse Village / 60 F1
   Tigh Nua an Dá Phota
Newbawn / *An Bábhún Nua* 53 C4
Newbliss / *Cúil Darach* 18 E4
Newbridge / *An Droichead Nua* 32 H1
   Co Galway / *Gaillimh*
Newbridge Co Limerick 49 D2
Newcastle / *An Caisleán Nua* 20 E3
   Co Down / *An Dún*
Newcastle Co Dublin 36 E4
Newcastle Co Galway 32 F3
Newcastle Co Tipperary 51 D5
Newcastle Co Wicklow 46 G1
Newcastle West / *An Caisleán Nua* 49 C3
Newcestown / *Baile Níos* 67 D1
Newcestown 68 E1
Newchapel 51 D4
Newferry 11 A2
Newinn / *Loch Ceann* 51 C3
Newmarket / *Áth Trasna* 59 D1
   Co Cork / *Corcaigh*
Newmarket Co Kilkenny 52 H3
Newmarket On Fergus / *Cora Chaitlín* 41 D5
Newmills Co Cork 67 D3
Newmills / *An Muileann Úr* 9 A1
   Co Donegal / *Dún na nGall*
Newmills / *An Muileann Nua* 10 H5
   Co Tyrone / *Tir Eoghain*

Newport / *Baile Uí Fhiacháin*	22	F2
Co Mayo / *Maigh Eo*		
Newport / *An Port Nua*	42	H5
Co Tipperary / *Tiobraid Árann*		
Newry / *An tIur*	19	B4
Newtown Co Galway	32	G4
Newtown Co Kildare	35	C3
Newtown Co Kilkenny	52	F1
Newtown Co Laois	45	A4
Newtown Co Limerick	50	G3
Newtown Co Mayo	22	H3
Newtown Co Meath	27	D3
Newtown Co Offaly	33	B5
Newtown Co Roscommon	33	A3
Newtown Co Roscommon	24	H4
Newtown Co Tipperary	51	A3
Newtown Co Tipperary	43	D3
Newtown Co Waterford	62	E2
Newtown Co Waterford	61	D3
Newtown Co Wexford	64	E3
Newtown Co Wexford	63	D4
Newtown Cashel / *Baile Nua an Chaisil*	33	C1
Newtown Cloghans / *An Baile Ur*	14	H5
Newtown Cunningham / *An Baile Nua*	3	A5
Newtown Forbes / *An Lois Breac*	25	D4
Newtown Gore / *An Dúcharraig*	17	B5
Newtown-Crommelin /	5	D5
Baile Nua Chromlain		
Newtownabbey / *Baile na Mainstreach*	12	E3
Newtownadam	51	C4
Newtownards / *Baile Nua na hArda*	12	G4
Newtownbutler / *An Baile Nua*	17	D4
Newtownhamilton / *Baile Úr*	19	A4
Newtownlow	34	F3
Newtownlynch	31	D5
Newtown Mt.kennedy /	46	G1
Baile an Chinnéidigh		
Newtown Sandes	49	A3
Newtownshandrum /	50	E4
Baile Nua Sheandroma		
Newtownstewart / *An Baile Nua*	9	D3
Nicholstown	53	A5
Ninemilehouse / *Tigh na Naoi Míle*	52	F3
Nobber / *An Obair*	27	C3
Nohaval / *Nuach a Bháil*	68	H1
North Ring	68	E2
Northlands / *An Táchairt Thuaidh*	27	B1
Noughaval Co Clare	41	D4
Nurney / *An Urnaí*	45	B5
Co Carlow / *Ceatharlach*		
Nurney Co Kildare	45	B1
Nutts Corner / *Coirnéal Nutt*	11	C4

O

Oaghley	48	H3
Oatfield	42	F5
O'Briensbridge	42	G5
O'Callaghansmills	42	F4
Oghill	33	A4
Ogonnelloe / *Tuath Ó gConáile*	42	G3
Oilgate / *Maolán na nGabhar*	54	E3
Old Head	68	G2
Old Kilcullen	45	C1
Old Kildimo	50	E1
Old Ross	53	B4
Old Town Co Laois	44	G3
Old Town / *An Seanbhaile*	33	B4
Co Roscommon / *Ros Comáin*		

Old Town Co Wexford	53	C2
Oldcastle / *An Seanchaisleán*	26	H3
Oldgrange	51	D5
Oldleagh	45	A3
Oldleighlin / *Seanleithghlinn*	45	A5
Oldtown Co Dublin	36	F1
Oldtown Co Roscommon	33	C3
Omagh / *An Ómaigh*	9	D4
Omeath / *Ó Meith*	19	C5
Onaght	30	E5
Oola / *Úlla*	51	A2
Oranmore / *Órán Mór*	31	D4
Oristown	27	B4
Orritor / *Na Coracha Beaga*	10	G4
Oughtdarra	40	F1
Oughter	34	E4
Oughterard / *Uachtar Ard*	30	H2
Oulart / *An tAbhallort*	54	E2
Outeragh	51	C4
Ovens / *Na hUamhanna*	60	F5
Owenbeg / *An Abhainn Bheag*	15	A3
Owenbristy	32	E5
Owning / *Ónainn*	52	G4

P

Palace / *An Phailís*	53	B3
Palatine	45	B4
Palatine Street	50	H2
Pallas Co Galway	32	H3
Pallas Co Laois	44	G2
Pallas Green / *An tSeanphailís*	50	H2
Pallas Green (New) / *Pailís Ghréine*	50	H2
Pallasboy	34	G3
Pallaskenry / *Pailís Chaonraí*	50	E1
Pallis	46	F5
Palmerston / *Baile Phámar*	36	E3
Park Co Wexford	64	E3
Park Co Mayo	23	C2
Parkacunna	60	H1
Parkbridge	45	D5
Parkgate	11	D3
Parkmore / *An Phairc Mhór*	31	D5
Parknasilla	58	E5
Parteen	42	F5
Partry / *Partraí*	22	H4
Passage	32	H1
Passage East	63	B3
Passage West / *An Pasáiste*	60	H5
Patrickswell / *Tobar Phádraig*	50	F2
Paulstown / *Baile Phóil*	53	A1
Peak	32	G4
Peterswell / *Tobar Pheadair*	42	F1
Pettigo / *Paiteagó*	9	A5
Pharis / *Fáras*	4	H4
Piercetown Co Cork	60	G4
Piercetown Co Wexford	54	E5
Pike	43	B1
Pike Corner	35	C1
Pike of Rush Hall / *An Paidhc*	44	E3
Piltown / *Baile an Phoill*	52	G4
Pluck	2	H5
Plumbridge / *Droichead an Phlum*	9	D2
Pollagh Co Galway	31	D5
Pollagh / *Pollach*	33	D4
Co Offaly / *Uíbh Fhailí*		
Pollatlugga	32	H4
Pollboy	33	A4
Pollshask	24	G5

Pomeroy / *Pomeroy*	10	F4
Pontoon	23	C1
Port	28	F3
Port Laoise	44	G2
Portacloy	13	D2
Portadown / *Port an Dúnáin*	19	B1
Portaferry / *Port an Pheire*	20	H1
Portaleen	3	C1
Portarlington / *Cúil an tSúdaire*	34	H5
Portavogie / *Port an Bhogaigh*	20	H1
Portballintrae / *Port Bhaile an Trá*	4	G2
Portglenone / *Port Ghluain Eoghain*	11	A1
Portland	43	A1
Portlaw / *Port Lach*	52	G5
Portmagee / *An Caladh*	57	B4
Portmarnock / *Port Mearnóg*	36	G2
Portmuck	12	F1
Portnablaghy / *Port na Bláiche*	2	F3
Portnashangan	26	G5
Portnoo / *Port Nua*	7	D2
Portraine	36	G1
Portroe / *An Port Rua*	42	H3
Portrush / *Port Rois*	4	F3
Portsalon / *Port an tSalainn*	2	H2
Portstewart / *Port Stiobhaird*	4	F3
Portumna / *Port Omna*	43	A1
Pottore	16	H5
Porturlin	13	D2
Poulanargid	59	D5
Poulnamucky	51	D4
Power's Cross / *Crois an Phaoraigh*	42	H1
Poyntz Pass / *Pas an Phointe*	19	B3
Priest Town	61	D1
Priesthaggard	53	B5
Prosperous / *An Chorrchoill*	35	C4
Puckaun / *Pocán*	43	A3

Q

Quarrytown	11	C1
Querrin / *An Cuibhreann*	48	H1
Quilty / *Coilte*	40	F4
Quin / *Cuinche*	42	E4

R

Radestown	44	H5
Raffrey / *Rafraidh*	20	F1
Raghly	15	C2
Rahaghy	26	H4
Rahara	33	A1
Rahan / *Raithean*	34	E4
Raharney / *Ráth Fhearne*	35	A1
Raheen Co Carlow	45	D4
Raheen Co Kerry	59	A2
Raheen Co Tipperary	51	C4
Raheen Co Westmeath	34	E2
Raheen / *An Ráithín*	53	C4
Co Wexford / *Loch Garman*		
Raheenagh	49	C4
Raheenlusk	54	F2
Rake Street	14	F5
Ramsgrange / *An Ghráinseach*	53	B5
Ranamackan	32	H5
Randalstown / *Baile Raghnaill*	11	B2
Rapemills	43	C1
Raphoe / *Ráth Bhoth*	9	B1
Rascalstreet	59	C1

Place	Ref	Place	Ref	Place	Ref
Rasharkin / *Ros Earcáin*	4 G5	Recess / *Sraith Salach*	30 E2	Rossaveel	30 F4
Rashedoge	2 G5	Reclain	10 F5	Rossbrin	66 H3
Ratcormack / *Ráth Chormaic*	61 A2	Redcastle	3 C3	Rosscahill / *Ros Cathail*	30 H3
Rath	43 D1	Redcross / *Chrois Dhearg*	46 G3	Rosses Point / *An Ros*	15 D2
Ráth Luirc (Charleville)	50 F4	Redgate	54 E3	Rossinver / *Ros Inbhir*	16 G2
Rathangan / *Rath Iomgháin*	35 A5	Redhills / *An Croc Rua*	17 D5	Rosslare / *Ros Láir*	54 E5
Rathanny	48 H5	Redwood	43 B1	Rosslare Harbour / *Calafort Rosláir*	54 F5
Rathaspick	26 E5	Renvyle	21 C5	Rosslea / *Ros Liath*	18 E3
Rathbrit	51 D3	Rerrin / *Raerainn*	66 F2	Rossmackowen	66 F2
Rathcabban / *Ráth Cabáin*	43 B1	Revallagh	4 G3	Rossmore Co Cork	67 D2
Rathcarran	27 B5	Rhode / *Ród*	34 H3	Rossmore / *An Ros Mór*	59 C5
Rathconor	25 A4	Richill / *Log an Choire*	19 A2	Co Cork / *Corcaigh*	
Rathconrath / *Ráth Conarta*	34 F1	Riesk	61 A3	Rossmore Co Laois	45 A4
Rathcool Co Cork	59 D2	Ring / *An Rinn*	64 G3	Rossmore Co Monaghan	18 F3
Rathcoole Co Dublin	36 E4	Ringaskiddy / *Rinn an Scidígh*	60 H5	Rossnowlagh / *Ros Neamhlach*	8 F5
Rathcore / *Ráth Cuair*	35 B2	Ringsend / *Droichead an Carraige*	4 E4	Rostellan / *Ros Tialláin*	61 A5
Rathcrony	40 H4	Ringstown	44 F2	Rostrevor / *Ros Treabhair*	19 C5
Rathdangan / *Ráth Daingin*	45 D3	Ringville / *An Rinn*	62 E3	Rosturk	22 E2
Rathdowney / *Ráth Domhnaigh*	44 E4	Rinnafarset	1 C4	Roundfort	23 C5
Rathdrum / *Ráth Droma*	46 F3	Rinneen Co Clare	40 F3	Roundstone / *Cloch na Rón*	29 D2
Rathduff	26 E5	Rinneen Co Cork	67 B3	Roundwood / *An Tóchar*	46 F1
Ratheenroe	66 H3	Rinville	31 D4	Rousky	10 E3
Rathernan	35 B4	Riverchapel	54 F1	Ruan / *An Ruán*	41 D3
Rathfeigh / *Ráth Faiche*	28 E5	Riverstick / *Áth an Mhaide*	68 G1	Rubane / *Rú Bán*	12 H5
Rathfilode	60 H3	Riverstown Co Cork	60 H4	Rush / *An Ros*	36 G1
Rathfriland / *Ráth Fraoileann*	19 D3	Riverstown / *Baile Idir dha Abhainn*	16 E4	Rusheen	59 D4
Rathfylane	53 C3	Co Sligo / *Sligeach*		Rusheeny	30 G2
Rathgarry	44 H4	Riverstown / *Baile Uí Lachnáin*	43 C1	Ryehill	32 F3
Rathgormuck / *Ráth Ó gCormaic*	52 F5	Co Tipperary / *Tiobraid Árann*		Rylane	60 E3
Rathgranagher	23 C5	Robertstown / *Baile Riobaird*	35 B4		
Rathkea	51 A3	Robinstown / *Baile Riobín*	27 C5		
Rathkeale / *Ráth Caola*	49 D2	Co Meath / *An Mhí*			
Rathkeevin	51 D4	Robinstown Co Wexford	53 D5		
Rathkenny / *Ráth Cheannaigh*	27 C4	Rochestown Co Kilkenny	52 H4		
Rathkeva	25 A3	Rochestown Co Kilkenny	53 A5		
Rathkineely	24 H3	Rochestown Co Tipperary	51 C5		
Rathlackan	14 G3	Rochfortbridge /	34 G2		
Rathlee / *Ráth Lao*	15 A3	*Droichead Chaisléan Loiste*			
Rathlyon	45 C4	Rockchapel / *Séipéal na Carraige*	49 C5		
Rathmaiden	62 F1	Rockcorry / *Buíochar*	18 F5		
Rathmelton / *Ráth Mealtain*	2 H4	Rockhill	50 F3		
Rathmore / *An Ráth Mhór*	59 B2	Rockmills	60 H1		
Co Kerry / *Ciarraí*		Rockstown	46 G3		
Rathmore / *An Ráth Mhór*	35 D5	Rodeen	25 B2		
Co Kildare / *Cill Dara*		Roevehagh	32 E5		
Rathmore Co Meath	27 B5	Rooaun	33 B5		
Rathmoylan Co Waterford	63 B4	Roonah Quay	21 D3		
Rathmoylon Co Meath	35 B2	Roosky Co Mayo	24 F1		
Rathmullan / *Ráth Maoláin*	2 H4	Roosky / *Rúscaigh*	25 C3		
Rathnamagh	14 G$	Co Roscommon / *Ros Comáin*			
Rathnew / *Ráth Naoi*	46 G2	Rooty Cross	33 B3		
Rathnure / *Ráth an Iúir*	53 C3	Rosapenna	2 G3		
Rathoma	14 G4	Rosbercon	53 A4		
Rathorgan	61 A3	Roscat	45 C4		
Rathowen	26 F5	Roscommon / *Ros Comáin*	25 A5		
Rathroeen	14 H4	Roscrea / *Ros Cré*	43 D3		
Rathruane	66 H3	Rosegreen / *Faiche Ró*	51 D3		
Rathtoe	45 C4	Rosemount	34 E2		
Rathvilly / *Ráth Bhile*	45 C3	Rosenallis / *Ros Fhionnghlaise*	44 F1		
Rathwire	34 H1	Rosmuck / *Ros Muc*	30 F3		
Ratoath / *Ráth Tó*	36 E1	Rosmult	51 C1		
Ratooragh	66 G3	Rosnakill / *Ros na Cille*	2 G3		
Ravensdale / *Gleann na bhFiach*	19 B5	Ross Behy	58 E2		
Ravernet / *Ráth Bhearnait*	11 D5	Ross Carbery / *Ros Ó gCairbre*	67 C3		
Ray / *An Ráith*	2 H4	Ross Port / *Ros Dumhach*	13 D3		
Reaghstown	27 D2	Ross West	22 H2		
Reananerree	59 B4	Ross / *An Ros*	26 G3		
Reanascreena / *Rae na Scríne*	67 C2	Co Meath / *An Mhí*			
Rear Cross / *Crois na Rae*	51 A1	Rossadrehid / *Ros an Droichead*	51 B4		
		Rossanean	58 H1		

S

Place	Ref
Saggart / *Teach Sagard*	36 E4
Saint Johnstown	9 C1
Saint Mullins	53 B3
Saintfield / *Tamhnaigh Naomh*	20 F1
Saleen	61 A5
Sallins / *Na Solláin*	35 C4
Sallybrook	60 H4
Sallypark	43 B4
Salthill	31 C4
Satlmills / *Muileann an tSáile*	63 C3
Sandholes / *Glais an Ghainimh*	10 G4
Sandyford / *Áth an Ghainimh*	36 F4
Santry / *Seantrabh*	36 F2
Saul	20 G2
Scardaun Co Mayo	23 D5
Scardaun Co Roscommon	33 A1
Scarriff / *An Scairbh*	42 G3
Scartaglin	59 A1
Scarva / *Scarbhach*	19 B2
Scotch Corner	18 G4
Scotch Street / *Sráid na hAlbanach*	19 A1
Scotshouse / *Teach an Scotaigh*	17 D5
Scotstown / *Baile an Scotaigh*	18 F3
Scrahan	48 F5
Scrahanfadda	59 A2
Scramoge / *Scramóg*	25 B4
Scrarour	60 H1
Screen / *An Scrín*	54 E3
Screggan / *An Screagán*	34 E4
Scriggan	3 D5
Scurlockstown	27 B4
Seaforde / *Baile Forda*	20 F2
Seapatrick	19 C2
Seskin	52 E4
Seskinore / *Seisceann Odhar*	9 D5
Shanacrane	67 B1

Shanagarry / *An Seangharraí* 61 B5
Shanaglish 42 E2
Shanagolden / *Seanghualainn* 49 C2
Shanahoe / *Seanchua* 44 F3
Shanballard 32 G3
Shanbally / *An Seanbhaile* 60 H5
  Co Cork / *Corcaigh*
Shanbally Co Galway 32 G1
Shanballyedmond 51 A1
Shanballymore / *An Seanbhaile Mór* 60 G1
Shangarry 32 H5
Shankill / *Seanchill* 36 G4
Shanlaragh / *Seanlárach* 67 C1
Shannakea / *Seanachae* 49 C1
Shannon 42 E5
Shannon Harbour / 33 C5
  Caladh na Sionainne
Shannonbridge / 33 B4
  Droichead na Sionainne
Shannonville 42 H3
Shanrahan 51 B5
Shanrath 49 D4
Shantonagh / *Seantonnach* 18 G5
Shanavogh 40 G4
Sharavogue / *Searbhóg* 43 C2
Shercock / *Searcóg* 27 B1
Sheskin 14 E4
Shevry 43 B5
Shillelagh / *Síol Ealaigh* 45 D5
Shinrone / *Suían Róin* 43 C2
Shrigley 20 G1
Shrone 48 H2
Shronell 51 A3
Shronowen / *Srón Abhann* 48 H2
Shrule / *Sruthair* 31 C1
Sillahertane 67 B1
Silver Bridge / *Béal Átha an Airgid* 19 A5
Silver Stream 18 F3
Silvermines / *Béal Átha Gabhann* 43 A4
Sion Mills / *Muileann an tSiáin* 9 C2
Six Crosses 48 H3
Six Road Ends 12 G4
Sixmilebridge / *Droichead Abhann* 42 E5
Sixmilecross / *Na Coracha Móra* 10 E5
Skahanagh 67 A1
Skahanagh North 60 H3
Skahanagh South 60 H3
Skeagh Co Cork 67 A3
Skeagh Co Westmeath 34 E1
Skehanagh Co Galway 32 F2
Skehanagh Co Galway 42 E1
Skeheen 51 A5
Skerries / *Na Sceirí* 28 G5
Skibbereen / *An Sciobairin* 67 B3
Skreen Co Meath 27 D5
Skreen / *An Scrín* 15 C3
  Co Sligo / *Sligeach*
Skull / *An Scoil* 66 H3
Slade 63 C4
Slane / *Baile Shlaine* 27 D4
Slieveroe / *Sliabh Rua* 53 A5
Sligo / *Sligeach* 15 D3
Smarmore 27 D3
Smithborough / *Na Mullaí* 18 E3
Smithstown 44 H4
Sneem / *An tSnaidhm* 58 E5
Sooey 16 E4
Spa / *An Spá* 48 F5
Spancelhill 41 D3
Spanish Point / *Rinnn na Spáinneach* 66 G4
Sperrin 10 F2

Spiddle 30 H4
Spink 44 H3
Spittaltown 34 E3
Spring Town 3 B5
Sraghmore 46 F1
Srah 13 C4
Srahanboy 44 E2
Sraheens / *Na Sraithíní* 23 C2
Srahmore / *An Srath Mór* 13 D4
Sruh 61 C1
St Margaret's 36 F2
Stabannan 28 E2
Stackallan / *Stigh Colláin* 27 D4
Staffordstown / *Baile Stafard* 11 B3
Stamullin 28 F5
Stapelstown 35 C3
Stepaside 36 F4
Stewartstown / *An Chraobh* 10 H4
Stillorgan 36 G4
Stone Bridge 18 E4
Stonepark 50 G2
Stonyford Co Antrim 11 D4
Stonyford / *Áth Stúin* 52 H2
  Co Kilkenny / *Cill Chainnigh*
Stormont 12 F4
Strabane / *An Strath Bán* 9 C2
Stabannan 28 E2
Stradbally Co Waterford 62 F2
Stradbally Co Kerry 47 D5
Stradbally / *An tSraidhbhaile* 44 H2
  Co Laois
Strade 23 C2
Stradone / *Sraith an Domhain* 26 H1
Straffan / *Teach Srafáin* 35 D4
Strahart / *Sraith Airt* 53 D1
Straid / *An tSraid* 12 E2
Strand / *An Trá* 49 C4
Strandhill / *An Leathros* 15 D3
Strangford / *Baile Loch Cuan* 20 G2
Stranocum / *Sraith Nócam* 4 H3
Stranorlar / *Srath an Urláir* 9 A2
Stratford / *Áth na Sreaiole* 45 C2
Streamstown Co Galway 29 C1
Streamstown / *Baile an tSruthain* 34 E2
  Co Westmeath / *An Iarmhí*
Street / *An tSráid* 26 F4
Strokestown / *Béal na mBuillí* 25 B3
Stroove 3 D2
Stuake 60 E3
Summer Cove 68 G1
Summerhill / *Cnoc an Linsigh* 35 C2
Suncroft / *Crochta na Gréine* 45 B1
Swan 44 H3
Swanlinbar / *An Muilcann Iarainn* 17 A4
Swatragh / *An Suaitreach* 10 H1
Swinford / *Béal Átha na Muice* 23 D2
Swords / *Sord* 36 F2

T

Taghmaconnell 33 A3
Taghmon / *Teach Munna* 53 D5
Taghshinny 26 E5
Tagoat / *Teach Gót* 54 F5
Tahilla 58 F5
Tallaght / *Tamhlacht* 36 E4
Tallanstown / *Baile an Tallúnaigh* 27 D2
Tallow / *Tulach an Iarainn* 61 B2
Tallowbridge 61 B2

Tamlaght / *Tamhlacht* 17 B2
  Co Fermanagh / *Fear Manach*
Tamlaght O'Crilly 11 A1
Tamnamore / *An Tamhnach Mhór* 10 H5
Tandragee / *Tóin re Gaoith* 19 B2
Tang / *An Teanga* 33 D1
Tankardstown 50 F4
Tara (Meath) 35 D1
Tara (Offaly) 34 E3
Tarbert / *Tairbeart* 49 A2
Tarmon / *An Tearmann* 49 A1
Tassagh / *An Tasach* 18 H3
Taur 59 C1
Tawnylea 16 G4
Tawny / *An Tamhnaigh* 2 G3
Tawnyinah 24 E2
Tedagh 66 H2
Tedavnet / *Tigh Damhnata* 18 F3
Teemore 17 C4
Teer 47 D5
Teeravane 57 B1
Teerelton / *Tír Eiltín* 59 D5
Teermaclane / *Tír Mhic Calláin* 41 D4
Teevurcher / *Taobh Urchair* 27 B2
Templeboy / *Teampall Baoith* 15 B3
Templecrum 52 G4
Templederry / *Teampall Doire* 43 B5
Templeetney 52 E4
Templemartin / *Teampall Mártan* 60 E5
Templemore / *An Teampall Mór* 43 D4
Templeoran 34 G3
Templepark 43 C3
Templepatrick / *Teampall Phádraig* 11 D3
Templeshanbo / *Teampall Seanbhoth* 53 C2
Templetouhy / *Teampall Tuaithe* 43 D4
Templetown 63 C3
Templeusque 60 H4
Tempo / *An tIompú Deiseal* 17 C2
Termon 2 G4
Termonbarry 25 C4
Termonfeckin / *Tearmann Feichin* 28 F3
Terryglass / *Tír Dhá Ghlas* 43 A1
Tevrin 34 H1
The Bush 28 F1
The Butts 45 A5
The Cross / *An Chrois* 3 B5
The Curragh / *An Currach* 35 B5
The Diamond / *An Diamant* 11 C4
  Co Antrim / *Aontroim*
The Diamond Co Tyrone 11 A4
The Downs / *Na Dúnta* 34 H1
The Drones 4 H4
The Dry Arch 4 H3
The Five Roads 36 F1
The Harrow 54 E2
The Heath 44 H1
The Leap 53 C4
The Loup / *An Lúb* 11 A3
The Pigeons / *Na Colúir* 33 D1
The Pike Co Tipperary 43 B2
The Pike Co Waterford 62 F2
The Rock / *An Charraig* 10 G4
The Rosses 1 C5
The Rower / *An Robhar* 53 B3
The Sheddings 11 D1
The Spa / *An Spá* 20 E2
The Sweep 52 G4
The Temple / *An Teampall* 12 E5
The Vee 51 C5
Thomastown / *Baile Mhic Andáin* 52 H2
  Co Kilkenny / *Cill Chainnigh*

Thomastown Co Limerick	50	H4
Thomastown Co Meath	27	B3
Thomastown Co Tipperary	51	B3
Thornton	45	C1
Three Castles	44	G5
Three Mile House	18	F4
Three Wells	46	F3
Thurles / Durlas	51	D1
Tibohine / Tigh Baoithán	24	G2
Tiduff	48	E3
Tikincor	52	E4
Timahoe Co Kildare	35	B3
Timahoe / Tigh Mochua Co Laois / Laois	44	H2
Tim Aoleague / Tigh Molaigte	68	E2
Timolin	45	B2
Tinehely / Tigh na hÉille	46	E4
Tinmuck	34	E3
Tinnakilla	53	D4
Tipperary / Tiobraid Árann	51	A3
Tirkane / Tír Chiana	10	H1
Tirnaneill	18	F3
Tirneevin	42	E1
Tober Co Cavan	16	G4
Tober Co Offaly	34	E3
Toberbeg	45	C2
Tobercurry / Tobar an Choire	15	C5
Toberelatan	32	F5
Tobermore / An Tobar Mór	10	H2
Tobernadarry	31	C1
Toberscanavan	15	D4
Toem / Tuaim	51	A2
Togher Co Cork	67	C1
Togher Co Louth	28	F3
Togher Co Meath	35	B2
Togher Co Offaly	34	H3
Togherbane	48	F4
Tomhaggard / Teach Moshagard	64	F3
Tonabrocky	31	C4
Tonlegee	22	G4
Tonyduff / An Tonnaigh Dhubh	27	A1
Toom / Tuaim	67	C1
Tooms	59	D5
Toomaghera	40	G2
Toomard / Tuaim Ard	32	G1
Toombeola	29	D2
Toome / Droichead Thuama	11	A2
Toomyvara / Tuaim Uí Mheára	43	B4
Tonregee	21	D1
Toor / An Tuar	43	A5
Tooraneena	61	D1
Tooraree	49	B2
Tooreen / Tuairín	60	G2
Tooreencahill	59	B1
Tooreendermot	49	C5
Toorgarriff	60	G2
Toorlestraun	15	B5
Toormakeady / Tuar Mhic Éadaigh	22	G5
Toormore / An Tuar Mór	66	G3
Torque	34	G3
Towergare	62	H1
Trabolgan	61	A5
Tracton	68	H1
Trafrask	66	G2
Tralee / Trá Lí	48	G5
Tramore / Trá Mór	62	H1
Trasternagh	32	F2
Trawlebane	67	A2
Trean	22	G5

Treantagh / Na Treantachta	2	G5
Trien / An Trian	24	G4
Trillick / Trileac	17	C1
Trim / Baile Átha Troim	35	C1
Trust	32	H3
Tuam / Tuaim	32	E1
Tuamgraney / Tuaim Gréine	42	G3
Tubber / An Tobar	42	E2
Tubbrid Co Kilkenny	44	F5
Tubbrid Co Tipperary	51	C5
Tulla / An Tulach Co Clare / An Clár	42	E3
Tulla Co Clare	41	D1
Tullagh	59	B5
Tullaghaboy	40	G4
Tullaghan / An Tulachán	16	E1
Tullagher / Tulachar	53	A3
Tullaghought	52	G4
Tullaherin	52	H2
Tullamore Co Kerry	48	H3
Tullamore / Tulach Mhór Co Offaly / Uíbh Fhailí	34	F4
Tullaree	48	E5
Tullaroan / Tulach Ruáin	52	F1
Tullassa	40	H4
Tullig Co Clare	48	F1
Tullig Co Kerry	48	H4
Tullig Co Kerry	58	F2
Tullow / An Tulch	45	C4
Tullyallen / Tulaigh Álainn	28	E4
Tullycanna	53	D5
Tullycoly	16	F4
Tully Cross	21	D5
Tullyhogue / Tulaigh Óg	10	H4
Tullylease	49	D5
Tullyroar Corner	18	H1
Tullyvin / Tulaigh Bhinn	18	E5
Tulrohaun / Tulach Shrutháin	24	E4
Tulsk / Tuilsce	25	A3
Tuosist / Tuath Ó Siosta	58	F5
Turin	34	H1
Turlough Co Clare	40	H1
Turlough / Turlach Co Mayo / Maigh Eo	23	C2
Turloughmore / An Turlach Mór	32	E3
Turnaspidogy	59	B5
Turnpike Cross	60	G1
Turreen	25	C5
Twomileborris / Buiríos Léith	51	D1
Tylas	35	D1
Tynagh / Tíne	32	H5
Tynan / Tuíneán	18	G2
Tyrella	20	F3
Tyrrellspass / Belach an Tirialaigh	34	G3

U

Unionhall / Breéantrá	67	C3
Upperchurch / An Teampall Uachtarach	43	B5
Upperlands / Áth an Phortáin	10	H1
Upton / Garraí Thancaird	68	F1
Urlaur / Urlár	24	F2
Urlingford / Áth na nUrlainn	44	E5

V

Vallymount / An Chrois	45	D1
Ventry / Ceann Trá	57	B1

Vicarstown / Baile an Bhoicáire	45	A1
Victoria Bridge / Droichead Victoria	9	C2
Villierstown / An Baile Nua	61	D2
Virginia / Achadh an Iuir	27	A3

W

Walterstown	27	D5
Ward / An Barda	36	F2
Waringstown / Baile an Bhairínigh	19	C1
Warrenpoint / An Pointe	19	C5
Watch House Cross Roads	35	D5
Watch House Village	45	D5
Waterfall / Tobar an Iarla	60	G5
Waterford / Port Láirge	52	H5
Watergrasshill / Cnocán na Biolraí	60	H3
Waterloo	60	F4
Waterville / An Coireán	57	C5
Wellingtonbridge / Droichead Eoin	53	C5
Wells	54	F2
Westport / Cathair na Mart	22	G3
Westport Quay	22	F3
Westtown	62	H2
Wexford / Loch Garman	54	E4
Wheelam Cross Roads	35	B5
White Gate Cross Roads	58	F1
White's Cross / Crois an Fhaoitigh	60	G4
Whiteabbey / An Mhainistir Fhionn	12	E3
Whitechurch / An Teampall Geal Co Cork / Corcaigh	60	G3
Whitechurch Co Wexford	53	A5
Whitecross / Corr Leacht	19	A3
Whitegate / An Geata Bán Co Clare / An Clár	42	H3
Whitegate / An Geata Bán Co Cork / Corcaigh	61	A5
Whitehall / An Baile Nua Co Roscommon / Ros Comáin	25	C4
Whitehall Co Westmeath	26	G5
Whitehead / An Cionn Bán	12	F2
Whites Town	28	G1
Whitesides Corner / An Phrochlais	11	B2
Wicklow / Cill Mhantáin	46	H2
Wilkinstown / Baile Uilcín	27	C4
Willbrook	40	H3
Williamstown / Baile Liam Co Galway / Gaillimh	24	G4
Williamstown / Baile Liam Co Westmeath / An Iarmhí	33	C2
Windgap / Bearna na Gaoithe	52	G3
Wolfhill / Cnocán na Mactíre	44	H3
Woodburn / Sruth na Coille	12	E3
Woodenbridge	46	F4
Woodford / An Ghráin	42	H1
Woodlawn	32	G3
Woodstown	63	B3

Y

Yellow Furze	27	D4
Youghal / Eochaill Co Cork / Corcaigh	61	C4
Youghal Co Tipperary	42	H3

NOTES

NOTES

NOTES